Active Server Pages Primer

The iSeries Definitive Guide to ASP

Active Server Pages Primer

The iSeries Definitive Guide to ASP

Mike Faust

First Edition

First Printing—May 2003

Every attempt has been made to provide correct information. However, the publisher and the author do not guarantee the accuracy of the book and do not assume responsibility for information included or omitted from it.

The following terms are trademarks of International Business Machines Corporation in the United States, other countries, or both: IBM, AS/400, OS/400, and 400. Other trademarked company names and product names mentioned herein are the property of their respective owners.

© 2003 MC Press Online, LP
ISBN: 1-58347-043-3

Corporate Offices:
125 N. Woodland Trail
Double Oak, TX 75077 USA
Sales & Customer Service
P.O. Box 4300
Big Sandy, TX 75755-4300 USA
www.mcpressonline.com

For information on translations or book distribution outside the USA or to arrange bulk-purchase discounts for sales promotions, premiums, or fund-raisers, please contact MC Press Sales Office at the above address.

Contents

Introduction

A t some point, you might have tried to create a simple Web page using just HTML. If so, you'll have discovered the downside to HTML coding: it is static. It doesn't allow you to create dynamically changing Web pages. This is where *Active Server Pages* (*ASPs*) come in.

This book takes an in-depth look at the ASP concept and how to make the most of it. You'll go step-by-step through creating entire applications using ASP. Along the way, you'll see correlations between the development process on the iSeries and the same process within an ASP. Once you've learned how easy it is to build applications in ASP, you might wonder how you ever got along without them.

Since HTML and ASP work hand-in-hand, chapter 1 provides an introduction to HTML. This chapter will help prepare you to learn Active Server Page programming. If you're already familiar with HTML, you can skip this chapter and start with chapter 2.

In chapter 2, you'll begin exploring the ASP concept, starting with the options for configuring a Web server to support ASPs. You'll examine what it takes to create an ASP and explore each of the special ASP objects. You'll also find basic examples of ASP scripts.

Chapter 3 shows how data access is achieved within an ASP. It explains the configuration requirements for creating a data access page, and then explains each of the objects used to connect to and read data from an iSeries database. In addition, you'll see how the process for reading data from the iSeries within an ASP correlates to the process used when programming in RPG on the iSeries. You'll also find ASP data-access examples in this chapter.

In chapter 4, you'll learn exactly how to go about converting an application from the iSeries into an ASP. The chapter explains the specific VB Script statements that replace RPG op codes, and then takes a broader look at how an interactive application in RPG would be converted into an ASP. You'll also explore how to use an ASP to replace printed reports with data displayed in a browser.

Chapter 5 takes you through the creation of a complete, fully functional, ASP "shopping cart" application. This example application reads, writes, and updates data on the iSeries from a Web-based order-entry system. You'll examine techniques used to pass data among multiple Web pages within a multi-page ASP application.

You'll go through the process of creating another complete ASP application in chapter 6. This time, it is an ad-hoc sales-reporting tool that uses data stored on the iSeries. Chapter 6 also shows how to use Microsoft Office Web Components to incorporate charts and spreadsheets into your ASP.

Chapter 7 looks at the changes Microsoft has implemented with ASP.NET, the next generation of Active Server Pages. Not only will this chapter help you understand the concept of .NET, you will also learn exactly what is required to convert an ASP application into an ASP.NET application.

To edit the ASP examples in this book, I recommend using the Microsoft Development Environment included with Visual Studio and Microsoft Office. Alternatively, you can use the Microsoft Script Debugger, which can be found by going to http://msdn.microsoft.com/scripting and choosing "Microsoft Script

Developer" in the Related Links area. Actually, any text editor can be used to edit ASP scripts, but the Microsoft Development Environment and the Microsoft Script Debugger give you enhanced editing capabilities, with some syntax-checking built in.

1

Creating HTML Web Pages

HTML (Hypertext Markup Language) is the backbone of all Web pages. Even with the introduction of newer technologies like Active Server Pages, Java, and Java Server Pages, HTML is still at the heart of every Web page on the Internet. For that reason, your exploration into the world of Active Server Pages starts with a little primer on using HTML tags to create Web pages. If you're already familiar with HTML, you can skip to chapter 2 to dive into Active Server Pages.

HTML Document Structure

HTML *tags* are the key components of all Web pages. Tags define all of the details of your page—everything from its background color, down to the font used for a specific section of text. HTML tags are identified by enclosing them between less-than and greater-than signs, as shown here:

```
<tagname>
```

Most tags require a tag-closing identifier, which is similar to using an ENDIF statement to identify the end of an IFXX group in RPG. Like an IFXX statement, HTML tags are often nested within one another. For example, the following tags identify an HTML table that has just one cell:

```
<TABLE WIDTH=100%>
   <TR WIDTH=50%>
      <TD>cell 1</TD>
   </TR>
</TABLE>
```

In this example, the <TR></TR> (table row) tags must be within a <TABLE></TABLE> group, and the <TD></TD> (table data) tags must be within a <TR></TR> group. All of the HTML tags that indicate how information is to be displayed within a page, along with any content that is to appear on the page, must be contained within the <BODY></BODY> group. (HTML is not case-sensitive, but its tag names are capitalized in the text of this book to distinguish them from JavaScript and VBScript reserved words.)

Document-Level Tags

Some HTML tags are used to define the attributes of your document. Within any Web page, the <HTML></HTML> tag group identifies the portion of the document that contains HTML. All HTML tags in your document must be contained in this group.

The two main subgroups within the <HTML> group are the <HEAD></HEAD> group, which defines header-level document information, and the <BODY></BODY> group mentioned earlier, which defines the displayable portion of the Web page. These tags support additional *attributes* that can be used in conjunction with them. For example, the <BODY> tag supports the following optional attributes:

- *TEXT*—Defines the default color for the text in a document.

- *LINK*—Defines the color used for the document's hyperlinks.

- *VLINK*—Identifies the color to be used for a hyperlink that was previously visited.

- *ALINK*—Sets the color to be displayed when a user clicks a hyperlink.

- *BGCOLOR*—Defines the background color for a document.

With this in mind, take a look at Figure 1.1. Here is the HTML code for that very basic Web page:

```
<HTML>
   <HEAD>
      <TITLE>My First Web Page</TITLE>
   </HEAD>
   <BODY BGCOLOR=BLACK TEXT=WHITE>
      This is my very first web page!
   </BODY>
</HTML>
```

Notice that each attribute is set using this format:

Attribute = value

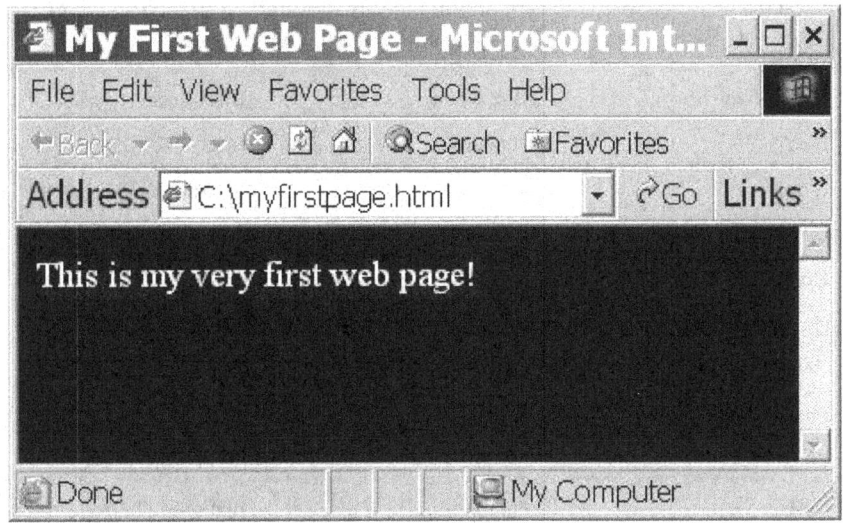

Figure 1.1: This simple Web page is created by just a few lines of HTML.

This will be the case with most attributes. Also notice that the values used for the two color attributes reference color names. However, they could also be specified in either of the following ways:

- Specify *RGB(red value, green value, blue value),* where each of the color values is a number from zero to 255 that identifies the amount of each color to be used. For example, RGB(0,0,0) represents black, while RGB(255,255,255) represents white.

- Use a pound sign (#) followed by the hexadecimal RGB value for the desired color.

Table 1.1 lists some common HTML color names, and their hex and RGB equivalents. These color definitions can be used with any of the HTML tags that support a color, not just the <BODY> tag.

Detail-level Tags

As the previous example illustrates, it is possible to create an HTML page using only header-level HTML tags. The resulting page, however, is just a text

Table 1.1: Examples of the Codes Used to Define Object Colors in HTM

Color Name	Hex Code	RGB Code
Blue	#0000FF	RGB(0, 0, 255)
Brown	#A52A2A	ARGB(245, 245, 220)
Dark Green	#006400	RGB(0, 100, 0)
Green	#00FF00	RGB(0, 255, 0)
Navy	#000080	RGB(0, 0, 128)
Orange	#FFA500	RGB(255, 165, 0)
Pink	#FFC0CB	RGB(255, 192, 203)
Purple	#A020F0	RGB(160, 32, 240)
Red	#FF0000	RGB(255, 0, 0)
Yellow	#FFFF00	RGB(255, 255, 0)

document with little or no formatting. With the use of additional HTML tags, you can add more interesting formatting to your page. For example, within the <HEAD></HEAD> element, you can use the <TITLE></TITLE> element to change the text that appears in the browser window's title bar. Any additional tags defined within the <HEAD></HEAD> element will not be displayed. The remaining detail-level tags are defined within the <BODY></BODY>element.

Detail-level elements allow you to control more minute details of your Web page. These tags let you do everything from defining font color and point size to displaying images. Many of these tags support their own unique attributes, which are used to further define the element on the page.

Defining Hyperlinks

One of the primary building blocks of an HTML document is the *hyperlink*, which provides a clickable link from one page to another, or even to a specific spot on a page. To control the definition of a hyperlink, use the <A> tag with the HREF attribute, as shown here:

```
<A HREF="http://www.mc-store.com/">MC Store</A>
```

Note the closing </A>, which defines the end of the hyperlink text. The text between the opening and closing tags will be displayed in the browser window as the hyperlink. The HREF value identifies the page to be loaded when a user clicks the hyperlink. In this example, we are referring to a Web server address. You can also refer to a specific document:

```
<A HREF="default.html">Default Link</A>
```

In this case, the page "default.html" would be loaded from the current server path. For example, if the Web server where this page was stored were named *Webserver*, this link would attempt to load "*http://Webserver/default.html.*"

The link in the HREF attribute doesn't have to be to an HTTP location; any registered document type can be referenced. For example, a hyperlink containing the *mailto:* prefix can be used to launch the user's mail client using the supplied e-mail address. For example, when a page containing the following code is loaded in the browser, a user can click the "Contact me" text to send an e-mail message to the specified address:

```
<A HREF="mailto:mikeffaust@yahoo.com">Contact me</A>
```

In addition to this, local file resources can be accessed through the use of the *file:* prefix. The following example creates a hyperlink labeled "Display File," which, when clicked, loads the file "anyfile.doc" from the user's local c: drive:

```
<A HREF="file:\\c:/anyfile.doc">Display File</a>
```

The <A HREF> tag can be used not only to define a hyperlink, but also to define the positional target for the link on a page. For example, the following hyperlink would instruct the browser to go to the target named "topic2" on the specified HTML document:

```
<A HREF="index.html#topic2">Go To Topic 2</A>
```

If you omitted the document name ("index.html") in this example, the browser would assume that the target is located on the current page.

To create a target location within a document, you also use the <A> tag, but you replace the HREF attribute with the NAME attribute. The following tag would create a target for the previous example:

```
<A NAME="topic2">TOPIC 2</A>
```

One other attribute of <A> is TARGET. This attribute defines the target frame or window where the document referenced in the HREF attribute will be loaded. (Frames are discussed later in this chapter.) For example, to cause the page in the HREF attribute to be loaded in a new browser window, you would set the TARGET attribute to "_blank":

```
<A HREF="http://www.mc-store.com" TARGET="_blank">MC Store</A>
```

When a user clicked on the hyperlink generated by this line of HTML source, a new browser window would be launched to display the page link.

Text-formatting Elements

There are many HTML elements that let you change the way text is displayed. One important point about text formatting in an HTML document, however, is that any extra lines are ignored. For example, the following segment:

```
<BODY> This is the page body </BODY>
```

would appear exactly the same as this one when displayed in a browser:

```
<BODY>
   This
   is
   the
   page
   body
</BODY>
```

To cause text to be displayed in a browser exactly as it is formatted within the document, you enclose it in the <PRE></PRE> element (which stands for "preformatted"). This element is often used within a Web page to define a section of program code. Here is an example of the <PRE></PRE> element:

```
<PRE>
This is line one of my page

This is line two of my page!!!

        This text is offset by 7 spaces.</PRE>
```

You can change the font in which text is displayed by using the <FONT></FONT> element. To change the color of the text, add the COLOR attribute to <FONT>. The value for this attribute is defined in the same way as the color attributes of <BODY> discussed earlier in this chapter.

The SIZE attribute of <FONT> sets the size of the text. You can specify it in one of two ways:

- As a value from one to seven. This value identifies a fixed size that may vary depending on the browser used to display the page.

- As a relative increase/decrease value, such as "+2" or "–1."

Finally, the FACE attribute identifies the name of the font to be used. To provide alternatives in case a particular font is not available on a client computer, include several names in a comma-separated string.

All three attributes of <FONT> can be used in combination, as shown here:

```
<FONT COLOR="RED" SIZE="+2" FACE="arial, helvetica">Test Text</FONT>
```

The line "Test Text" would be displayed in red, two sizes larger than the default text size for the document, using Arial or Helvetica (depending on which one is available on the client computer).

To make text appear bold or italicized, place it within the <B></B> or <I></I> elements, respectively. These elements can be used independently or in combination with one another, as shown here:

```
<B>Bold Text</B>
<I>Italicized Text</I>
<B><I>Bold Italicized Text</I></B>
```

In addition to these text-formatting elements, the text can be changed to one of six predefined heading styles based on the browser displaying the page. This is done using the <H*n*></H*n*> element, where *n* is a number from one to six. Text placed within the <H1></H1> element would be shown in the largest heading size, while text contained within the <H6></H6> element would be shown in the smallest. These elements, too, can be combined with the other text-formatting elements. For example, consider these lines of HTML:

```
<H1>This is <I>heading 1</I> text</H1>
<H2><I>This</I> is heading 2 text</H2>
```

Within the first line, the text "heading 1" would be italicized, while in the second line, the word "This" would be italicized. When displayed in the browser, these two lines would appear as shown in Figure 1.2.

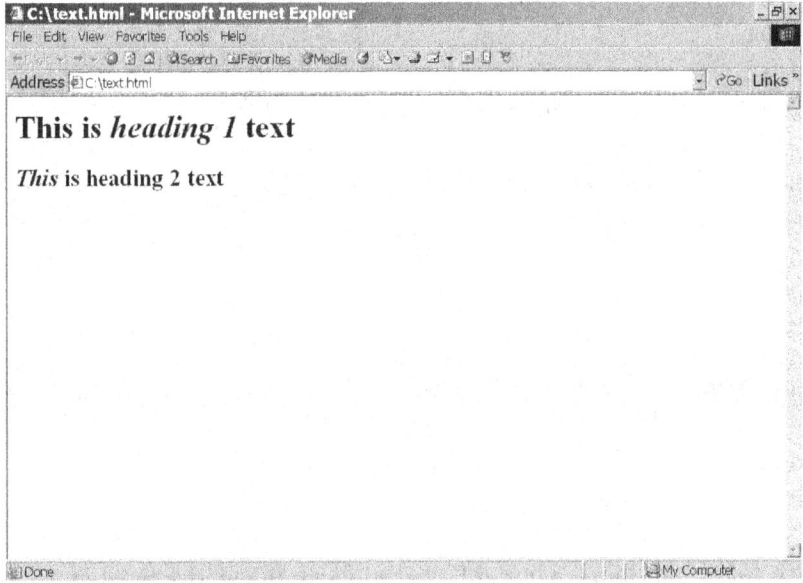

Figure 1.2: Heading styles can be combined with other elements to change text appearance.

Paragraph Formatting

In addition to being able to change the look of your text, you can also define the line and paragraph formatting using several HTML elements. The <P></P> element defines a paragraph of text. Placing text within this element will cause that text to be kept together when the page is displayed in a browser. This element supports the ALIGN attribute, which identifies the horizontal alignment for the text within the paragraph as either left, right, center, or justify.

You can use the <BR> element to force a line break within your text. For example, the following HTML source would be displayed as two lines in the browser window:

```
<P ALIGN="CENTER">This is line one<BR>and this is line 2</P>
```

Notice that the <BR> element does not include a closing (</BR>) tag. This is because the element is not used to define a section of text, but to simply insert a line break. This is one of a few HTML elements that do not require a closing tag.

The <BLOCKQUOTE></BLOCKQUOTE> element defines a section of text that is to be offset from other text when displayed in the browser. The following example combines the <BLOCKQUOTE></BLOCKQUOTE> element within the <P> element:

```
<P ALIGN="LEFT">This text is part of the standard paragraph<BR>

<BLOCKQUOTE>While this text<BR> is offset with larger margins<BR>
          than other text in our page</BLOCKQUOTE><BR>

This text returns to <BR>normal margins</P>
```

In this example, all of the text will be left-aligned. When displayed in the browser, it will appear as shown in Figure 1.3.

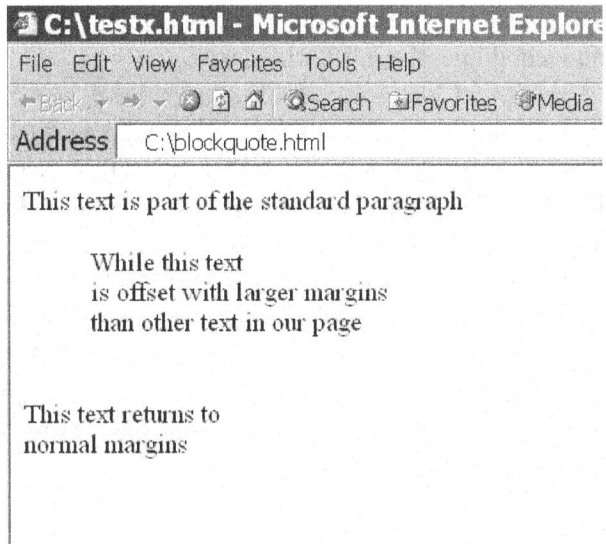

Figure 1.3: This example uses the <BLOCKQUOTE> element to offset some of the text.

The <DIV></DIV> element creates logical divisions within a document. Like the <P></P> element, this element supports the ALIGN attribute. It also supports the COLOR attribute, which can be used to define the font color for text within the element. This element is widely used to create a logical grouping of text and other HTML elements, such as images. These logical groupings can then be accessed as a single entity from a client JavaScript or VBScript function. (You'll learn more about this a little later in the book.)

Graphic Elements

Of course, there's more to HTML pages than just text. Graphic elements allow you to create more interesting HTML pages. The <IMG> element displays an image file (JPEG, GIF, etc.) within your document. Its SRC attribute identifies the location of the file containing the image, as shown in the following two lines:

```
<IMG SRC="picture.jpg">

<IMG SRC="http://www.mywebserver.com/image.gif">
```

In the first line, the location for SRC is specified as a relative path to the HTML document. In the second line, the full URL is used.

In addition to the SRC attribute, <IMG> also supports the ALIGN attribute, which again defines horizontal alignment, and the BORDER attribute, which defines the width of the border displayed around the image. To eliminate the border altogether, set BORDER to zero.

The <IMG> element can be placed within a hyperlink (<A HREF>) tag to cause the image to act as a hyperlink. This allows you to use an <IMG> element like an icon within your document. For example, the following source would display the image file named "image.gif" and allow the user to click on the image to load the HTML page "page2.html":

```
<A HREF="page2.html"><IMG SRC="image.gif"></A>
```

In addition to including image files, you can also insert a simple horizontal line in your page using the <HR> element. The height of the line is defined using the SIZE attribute. This value is specified as the number of pixels. The line width is defined using the WIDTH attribute, which is also defined as number of pixels or as a percent of the page width. The optional NOSHADE attribute can be included to remove the line shadow, which is included by default. The following example would create a line that is 50% of the available browsers space in width, and 5 pixels in height, with no shadow:

```
<HR SIZE=5 WIDTH=50% NOSHADE>
```

This element does not require a closing tag.

HTML Tables

Tables are one of the most widely used features of HTML. Not only are they used to display data in rows and columns, but they can also give your Web page a more appealing look. The main element used to create an HTML table is

<TABLE></TABLE>. This element identifies the overall size and look of a table. It supports some attributes that you've already seen, like BGCOLOR to define the table's background color and BORDER to define the table's border width.

The <TABLE></TABLE> element also supports several other attributes. The CELLPADDING attribute defines the amount of empty space displayed between the cell border and the table data. The CELLSPACING attribute is similar, but defines the amount of space between cells in a table.

The HEIGHT and WIDTH attributes define the overall size of the table. These two attributes can be defined as either a fixed number of pixels or as a percent of the available page space, as with the <HR> element discussed earlier. HEIGHT and WIDTH are defined in terms of page space rather than page width or height because you can embed one table within another. For example, if a table has a width of 50% and contains a second table with a width of 50%, the second table will be 25% of the total page width. This is shown in Figure 1.4.

Within the <TABLE></TABLE> element, several other elements define the rows and columns of the table. The <TR></TR> element identifies a single row in a table. This element supports the BGCOLOR attribute, which will define the row's background color. The <TR></TR> element also supports the ALIGN and VALIGN attributes, which are used to define horizontal and vertical alignment, respectively. The ALIGN attribute is used in the same way as for the <FONT></FONT> element discussed earlier. The VALIGN element defines

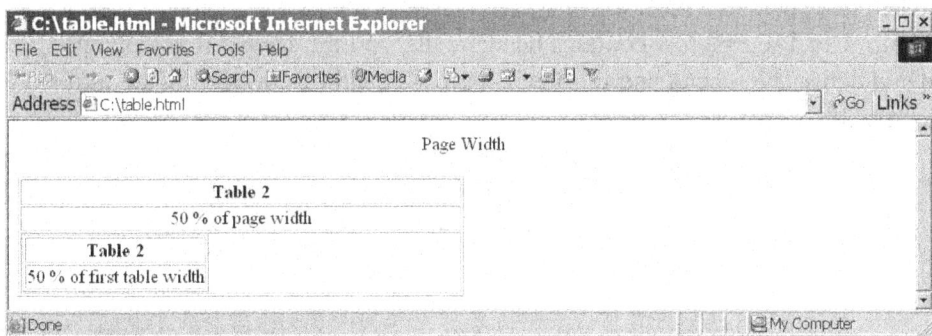

Figure 1.4: The widths of nested tables are defined as a percentage of available space.

the vertical alignment of text within the current row as either top, middle, or bottom.

Within the <TR></TR> element, you define cells using the <TH></TH> or <TD></TD> element. The <TH></TH> element indicates a table heading. Text in heading cells is displayed in bold. The <TD></TD> element identifies table data cells. Both of these elements support the BGCOLOR attribute to define the cell's background color, the WIDTH attribute to define the cell's width, and the ALIGN attribute to define the cell's alignment. In addition, both of these elements support the ROWSPAN and COLSPAN attributes, which allow a cell to span multiple rows or columns within a table.

The following HTML source would create a simple table:

```
<TABLE WIDTH=90% BGCOLOR="LightSkyBlue" BORDER=1>
   <TR VALIGN=TOP>
      <TH ALIGN="CENTER"> COLUMN 1 </TH>
      <TH ALIGN="RIGHT">Column 2</TH>
      <TH ALIGN="LEFT">Column 3</TH>
   </TR>
   <TR VALIGN=BOTTOM>
      <TD> Data Cell 1</TD>
      <TD ALIGN="CENTER" COLSPAN=2>Data Cells 2 & 3</TD>
   </TR>
</TABLE>
```

When displayed in a browser, this source creates the two-row table shown in Figure 1.5. The first row contains header cells, and the second row contains detail cells. The second and third cells in the second row are combined into a single cell.

COLUMN 1	Column 2	Column 3
Data Cell 1	Data Cells 2 & 3	

Figure 1.5: This is an example of an HTML table.

As mentioned earlier, you can embed one table within another to add complexity to the page. Figure 1.6 provides the HTML source for an example of embedded tables.

This example creates one table within another table. The embedded table has a border, while the main table has no border. The output resulting from this HTML is shown in Figure 1.7.

As you'll see through the examples in this book, in addition to displaying data, HTML tables can also be used to format Web pages. A good example of this would be using a table to create columns of text, as for a newspaper.

```
<TABLE WIDTH=50% BORDER=0>
   <TR VALIGN=TOP>
      <TD WIDTH=50%>Cell 1
         <TABLE WIDTH=100% BORDER=1>
            <TR>
               <TD>Sub Cell 1</TD>
               <TD>Sub Cell 2</TD>
               <TD>Sub Cell 3</TD>
            </TR>
            <TR>
               <TD>Sub Cell 4</TD>
               <TD>Sub Cell 5</TD>
               <TD>Sub Cell 6</TD>
            </TR>
            <TR>
               <TD>Sub Cell 7</TD>
               <TD>Sub Cell 8</TD>
               <TD>Sub Cell 9</TD>
            </TR>
         </TABLE>
      </TD>
      <TD> Cell 2</TD>
   </TR>
   <TR VALIGN=BOTTOM>
      <TD> Cell 3</TD><TD ALIGN="CENTER" COLSPAN=2>Cell 4</TD>
   </TR>
</TABLE>
```

Figure 1.6: HTML tables can be embedded within one another.

19

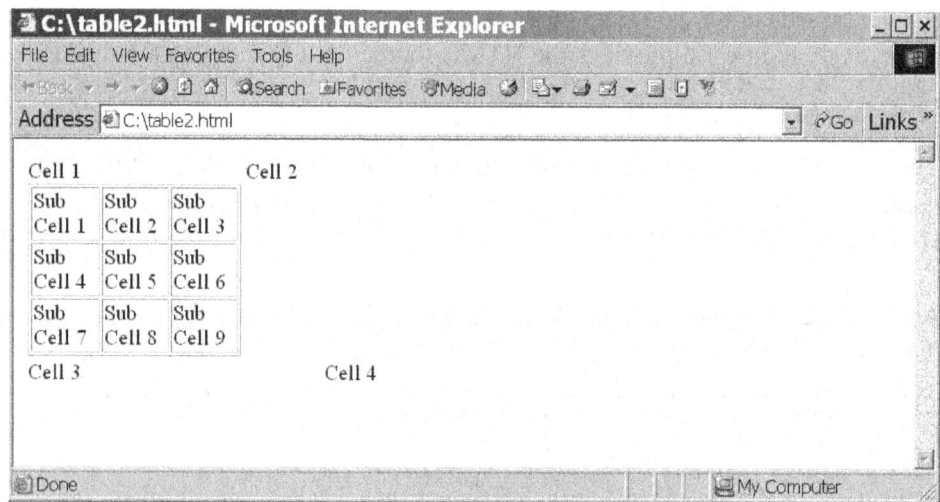

Figure 1.7: This is an example of a nested table.

HTML Forms

One of the keys to creating interactive Web pages is using HTML forms. Form tags define input elements such as text boxes, list boxes, radio buttons, check boxes, and even command buttons. When defining HTML forms, the base element is <FORM></FORM>. This is used to identify the name of the form itself and how the form is to be used. Three main attributes are required when defining the <FORM></FORM> element:

- The NAME element identifies the name by which the form will be accessed.

- The ACTION attribute defines what is to be done with the form. This attribute can be the name of a Web page that will read the values from the form, or the name of a client VBScript or JavaScript function that will process the form data.

- The METHOD attribute identifies how the data is passed to other applications. This attribute is defined as either GET, which indicates that values are sent as part of the URL through a query string, or POST, which passes the values to the next page without using the query string.

20

You'll learn more about these attributes in later chapters. For now, it's enough to know that a standard form-element definition would look something like this:

```
<FORM NAME="MYFORM" ACTION="http://myserver/process.asp" METHOD=GET>
   … other form elements defined
</FORM>
```

In this example, a form named MYFORM would send its values through a query string to the page "process.asp."

Within the form definition, you define other elements to create the form's fields, in the same way you use DDS to define a display file on the iSeries. The primary element used in forms is <INPUT>, which does not require a closing tag. This one element can be used to define many different types of objects, from check boxes to text boxes, depending on the value of its TYPE attribute. Table 1.2 lists the valid object types and their descriptions.

The TEXT input type creates a simple text-input field. The following example would define a text field named TEXT1 that would show the value specified in the VALUE attribute when the form is initially displayed:

Table 1.2: Valid TYPE Values of the <INPUT> Element

TYPE Value	Description
BUTTON	Creates a standard command button. This will not automatically submit the form.
CHECKBOX	Adds a checkbox to the form.
IMAGE	Displays an image file which, when clicked, will act as a submit button.
RADIO	Displays a radio button on the form.
RESET	Appears as a command button that resets the form fields to their original values.
SUBMIT	Displays a command button that is used to submit the form.
TEXT	Creates a simple text-input box.

```
<INPUT TYPE="TEXT" NAME="TEXT1" VALUE="Sample Text">
```

Radio buttons are normally used to define a set of options, only one of which can be selected. You do this in an HTML form by defining several <INPUT> elements that all have the same value for their NAME attribute, but different values for their VALUE attributes. The following example would display three radio buttons that are part of the same group:

```
<INPUT TYPE=RADIO NAME="CHOICES" VALUE="1" CHECKED>Option 1<BR>
<INPUT TYPE=RADIO NAME="CHOICES" VALUE="2">Option 2<BR>
<INPUT TYPE=RADIO NAME="CHOICES" VALUE="3">Option 3<BR>
```

When displayed in the browser, this would result in three radio buttons. Only one of these may be selected at one time. The CHECKED attribute identifies that the button containing that attribute will be selected by default. When displayed in the browser, these buttons would appear as shown in Figure 1.8.

The CHECKBOX input type works like RADIO, except that each check box has a unique NAME attribute and does not have a definable value. Instead, it will return a value of "on" if it is checked. A check box would be defined as shown here:

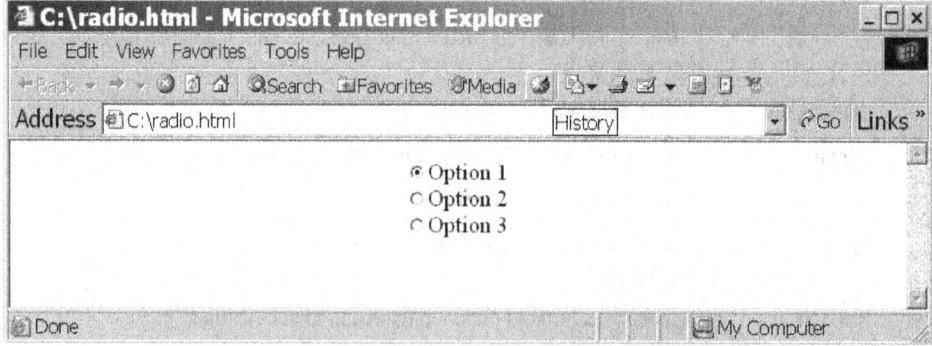

Figure 1.8: This radio-button group is part of an HTML form.

```
<INPUT TYPE="CHECKBOX" NAME="BOX1" CHECKED>Select This<BR>
```

Figure 1.9 shows a sample of how this check box would be displayed in a Web browser.

The BUTTON, SUBMIT, and RESET input types display different kinds of command buttons. SUBMIT creates a button that can be used to send the form values to the page defined on the form's ACTION attribute. The SUBMIT button's NAME attribute identifies the button. Its VALUE attribute serves the following two purposes:

1. Defines the text to appear on the command button.

2. Identifies the value to be passed through the variable defined on the *NAME* attribute.

You can have multiple SUBMIT buttons on one form. These buttons can either all use the same name, or can have their own unique names. The source shown below would display a SUBMIT button labeled "Process Page" on a form:

```
<INPUT TYPE="SUBMIT" NAME="BUTTON1" VALUE="Process Page">
```

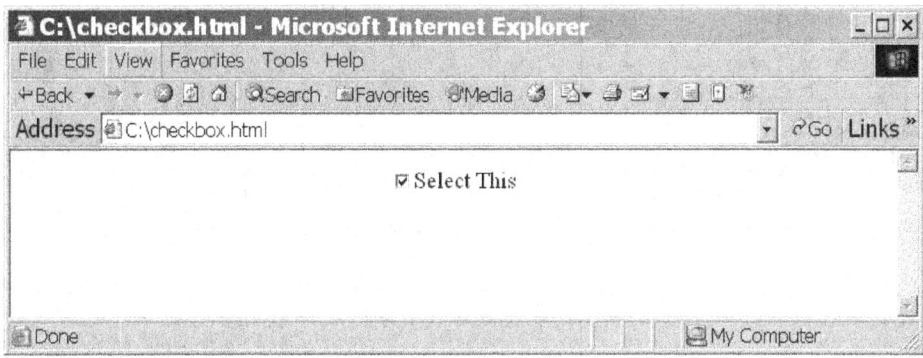

Figure 1.9: The CHECKBOX input type appears this way in the browser.

The RESET input type works like SUBMIT, except that rather than submitting the form, RESET returns the form variables to their original values. The following line would define this kind of button:

```
<INPUT TYPE="RESET" NAME="BUTTON2" VALUE="Reset Form">
```

When displayed on the page, this would appear identical to the SUBMIT button, except it would be labeled "BUTTON2" instead of "BUTTON1."

Finally, the BUTTON input type creates a button that doesn't have any automatic function. This type of button launches the function defined by the element's ONCLICK attribute. For example, the following line of HTML would display a command button labeled "Some Other Command" that, when clicked, would launch a JavaScript function called MyFunction:

```
<INPUT TYPE=BUTTON NAME="BUTTON3" VALUE="Some Other Command"
        ONCLICK="Javascript:MyFunction();">
```

Figure 1.10 shows how all three of these buttons would look in a browser. Although they all appear to be the same type of object, each one would function differently.

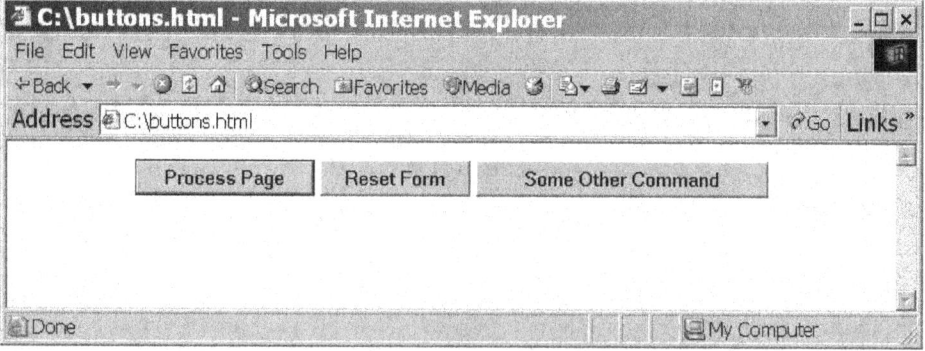

Figure 1.10: Three different types of command buttons can be defined using the <INPUT> element.

The IMAGE input type displays an image in the browser, like the <IMG> element discussed earlier. An IMAGE object, however, will function as a SUBMIT button when clicked. An <INPUT> element that has a type of IMAGE supports the SRC attribute, which is used to define the location of the image file to be displayed. The following source would create an IMAGE input type:

```
<INPUT TYPE=IMAGE SRC="IMAGE1.JPG" NAME="IMAGEBUTTON">
```

When this object is displayed, the user would be able to click on the image to submit the form. In most cases, this input type is used to create a "custom" button for submitting forms. The values returned when this element is selected represent the horizontal and vertical positions of the mouse cursor. These values are returned through $.x$ and $.y$ properties for the element. In the example above, the horizontal position would be read by accessing the form variable IMAGE.x.

In addition to the <INPUT> elements, the <SELECT></SELECT> element can be used to create an input list box on the form. The <SELECT></SELECT> element supports a NAME attribute that identifies the name by which the object is accessed. An optional MULTIPLE attribute can be included to indicate that more than one value in the list can be selected. You define each of the items within a list box using the <OPTION></OPTION> element. This element supports a VALUE attribute, which defines the value to be returned in the variable when the item is selected. This element also supports a SELECTED element, which identifies whether or not an option is selected within the list box. The value to be displayed within the list box is defined between this element's two tags.

The follow source would be used to define a list box:

```
<SELECT NAME="LISTBOX1">
    <OPTION VALUE="Y">Yes</OPTION>
    <OPTION VALUE="N">No</OPTION>
</SELECT>
```

This HTML source defines a list box with "Yes" and "No" options. While these values are displayed in the list box, a value of "Y" or "N" will be returned in the LISTBOX variable as defined on the VALUE property.

The <TEXTAREA></TEXTAREA> element is similar to a text <INPUT> element. The difference is that a text area is made up of multiple lines of text. This element supports the NAME attribute, which identifies the name by which the element is accessed. It also supports the ROW and COLS elements, which define the number of character rows and columns that the element will display. The value for the text area is defined between the opening and closing tags, as shown here:

```
<TEXTAREA NAME="MYTEXT" ROWS=10 COLS=20>
   This is a sample text area.

   This can contain multiple lines of text which will be displayed
   in a single box. This text will be passed through the form or
   querystring variable identified on
   the NAME attribute.
</TEXTAREA>
```

Unlike the text contained within the rest of an HTML page, this text will be displayed as it is formatted. Carriage returns will be honored as they are entered. Figure 1.11 shows what this text area looks like in a browser.

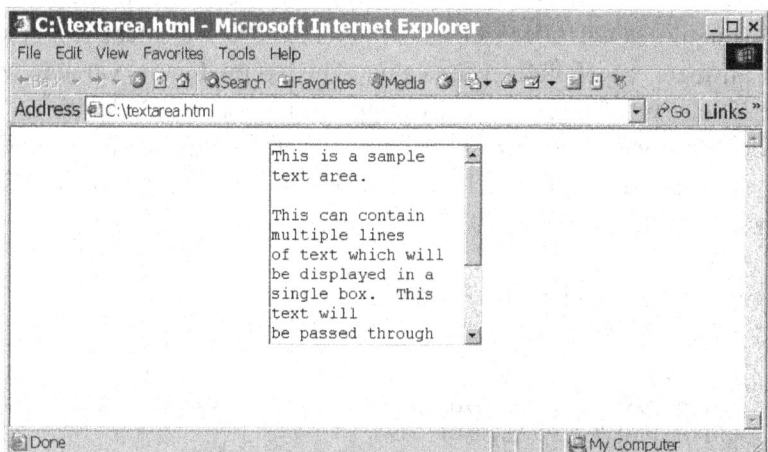

Figure 1.11: This is a how a TEXTAREA element looks in a Web browser.

HTML Frames

Framed HTML documents allow you to divide the browser window to display multiple Web pages. For example, you might have a screen that has a menu along its top portion. When an option is selected from the menu, a different document is loaded in the lower portion of the screen. The primary element used to create a framed HTML page is <FRAMESET></FRAMESET>. This element defines a group of HTML frames that are displayed on a single screen.

You identify the number of frames within the frame set using the ROWS and COLS attributes. ROWS identifies the number of frames oriented vertically, while COLS defines the number to display horizontally. Both of these values can be specified as either an absolute number of pixels, or as a percent of the total screen size. This value must be specified for each frame to be created. For example, to create a page with three horizontal frames, you might set COLS = "50%, 25%, 25%". In this case, the first frame would take up 50% of the screen, and the other two would each take up 25%.

The FRAMEBORDER attribute is defined as "Yes" or "No" to identify whether or not a visible border is displayed around the frame. Along with this attribute, the BORDER attribute defines the width of the border displayed. The FRAMESPACING attribute defines the amount of space left between each frame in the frame set. As with tables, HTML frames can be embedded within one another, so you could create a page with, say, three frames across the top half of the screen and two frames along the bottom.

The definition of each frame in a frame set is specified using the <FRAME> element. This element's SRC attribute identifies the URL of the document to be displayed within the frame. The NAME attribute uniquely identifies the frame within the frame set. This value can be used on the TARGET attribute of the <A></A> element to identify a target frame for a document to be loaded through a hyperlink. The <FRAME> element's SCROLLING attribute accepts values of "Yes," "No," or "Auto" to define whether or not scroll bars should be displayed within the frame if the document is too large for it. A value of "Yes" or "No" is absolute, while a value of "Auto" will display scroll bars if required. If the NORESIZE attribute is present, a user cannot change the size of the frame on the page. The MARGINWIDTH and MARGINHEIGHT attributes define the amount of space left around this frame. Last but not least, the <NOFRAMES></NOFRAMES> element defines what should be displayed if a user's browser does not support HTML frames.

The source shown in Figure 1.12 gives an example of a framed document definition. Notice the value "1*" within the COLS and ROWS definitions in Figure 1.12. This tells the browser to use the remaining unused portion of the screen for the frame being defined. Also, the <FRAMESET></FRAMESET> definitions fall outside of the <HEAD></HEAD> and <BODY></BODY> elements, but within the <HTML></HTML> element.

The example in Figure 1.12 would create the embedded frame set shown in Figure 1.13. The text within the <NOFRAMES></NOFRAMES> element would be displayed in browsers that don't support frames.

As mentioned earlier, you can reference any of these frames from a hyperlink. For example, the following <A></A> element would cause the page to be loaded in the left, bottom frame of Figure 1.13:

```
<A HREF="newint.html" TARGET="int">Load New Page</A>
```

```
<html>
<frameset rows="75,1*" frameborder="NO" border="0" framespacing="0">
    <frame name="top" scrolling="NO" src="top.html"  noresize>
        <frameset cols="1*,25%" frameborder="YES" border="1"
        framespacing="0">
            <frame name="int" scrolling="auto" src="int.html">
            <frame scrolling="auto" name="doc" src="doc.html">
        </frameset>
</frameset>
<noframes>
    <body bgcolor="#FFFFFF">
        Your browser does not support frames.
    </body>
</noframes>
</html>
```

Figure 1.12: *This sample HTML creates a framed document.*

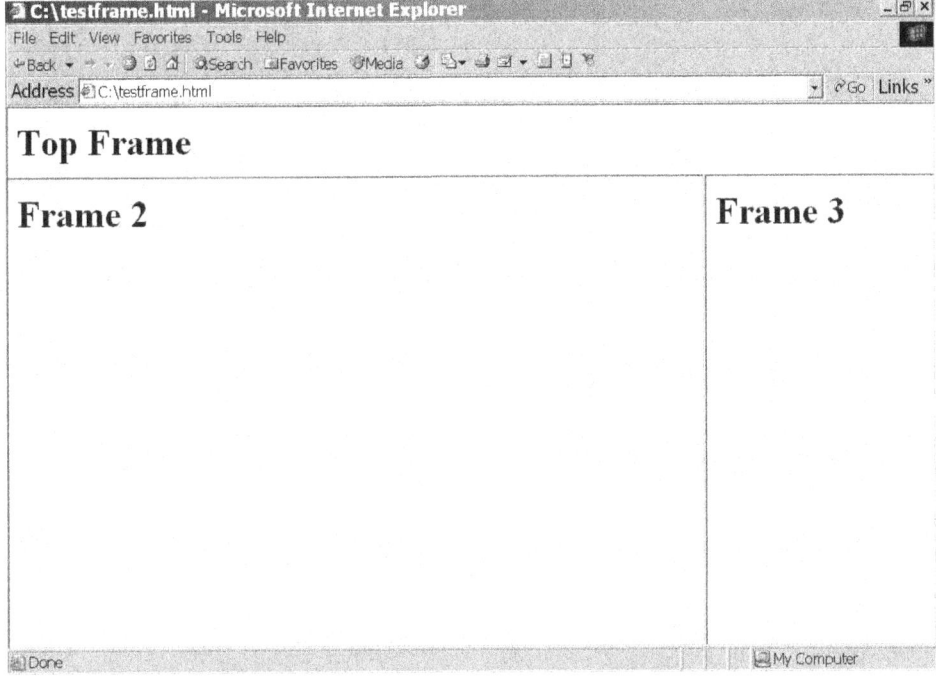

Figure 1.13: This is a sample of a framed Web page.

When a user clicks on the hyperlink labeled "Load New Page," the "newint.html" file would load into the defined frame.

There are differing opinions on the usefulness of HTML frames. At one time, there was a great movement toward using framed HTML documents. More recently, things have gone the other way, and people have started to move away from using frames. The choice is up to you; it might ultimately depend on the application you are developing.

Summary

While this chapter is by no means a complete guide to HTML, it does give you some of the tools you'll need to start learning Active Server Page programming. For more information on HTML, your best resource is the Web site of the World Wide Web consortium, which can be found at *www.w3.org*.

2

Introduction to Active Server Pages

Active Server Pages were introduced by Microsoft in 1996 as a download-able feature of Internet Information Server 3.0. The concept is pretty simple: an Active Server Page allows code written in the JavaScript or VBScript languages to be embedded within the HTML tags of a Web page and executed on the Web server. There are great advantages to this, not the least of which is security. Since your code is executed on the Web server, only HTML tags are sent to the browser. The result is that the ASP code is "invisible" to the end user.

Another upside to the "server-side script" concept is that it allows things like database connections to be made from the Web server rather than from the client. Therefore, any special configurations that might need to be set up, like ODBC data sources, only have to exist on the server. Of course, before you can create an Active Server Page (ASP), you'll need to look at the software requirements.

The Setup

Before you can create an Active Server Page, you'll need a Web server that sup-ports Active Server Pages. The most obvious choice would be Microsoft's

Internet Information Server (IIS) version 3.0 or higher. IIS is available for Windows NT 4.0 or higher as part of the Windows NT option pack, which can be downloaded from Microsoft's Web site. For the highest level of compatibility and functionality, you'll want to use the most recent version of IIS.

Another option that you might not have considered is Microsoft's Personal Web Server for Windows 9x and Windows ME. If you're running Windows 98, Personal Web Server can be installed by running "setup.exe" from the Windows 98 setup CD under the "\add-ons\pws\" folder. Alternatively, it can be downloaded from Microsoft's Web site as part of the Windows NT option pack. This download is the only choice for Windows 95 or Windows ME. It's important to note that Microsoft does not support running Personal Web Server under Windows ME. While Personal Web Server is not the optimal choice for a production Web server, it is a great option for developing and testing your ASP scripts.

If you're running IIS or Personal Web Server, no additional software is required to support Active Server Pages. To allow a user to access an ASP, the ability to do so must be enabled on the IIS server. This is done by selecting "Scripts" or "Execution (Including Scripts)" from the "Home Directory" tab of the Properties window for your Web site, as shown in Figure 2.1.

For other operating systems or Web servers, it gets a little tricky, but is possible. For Unix or Linux servers running the Apache Web server, you can use a bolt-on product to add ASP support. Sun Microsystems' Sun ONE Active Server Pages (formerly called Chili!Soft ASP) is one of these products. This product supports most, but not all, of the controls available in IIS. This is just one product that can add Active Server Page support to non-Microsoft Web servers. Table 2.1 has a more complete list of ASP compatibility products and the operating systems and Web servers they run on.

There are products to allow ASPs to be used on just about any Web server out there. This fact makes using ASPs that much more attractive because you aren't limited in the choice of hardware, operating system, or Web server to host your Web pages. As you can see, there are even ASP-compatibility products for the iSeries.

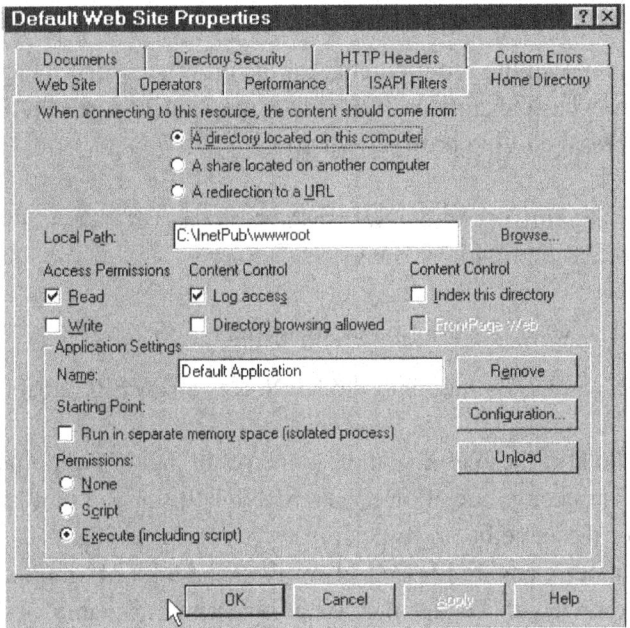

Figure 2.1: Active Server Pages are enabled by adding script permission.

Table 2.1: Compatibility Products for Using ASP on Non-IIS Web Servers

Product Name	Manufacturer	Web Servers Supported	Operating Systems
Sun ONE Active Server Page	Sun Microsystems	iPlanet, Apache, and Zeus	Solaris, Linux, Windows, and HP-UX
Instant ASP	STRYON	Apache, Oracle	Linux, Novell Netware, Sun IBM
		MS Internet Information Server (IIS), BEA	Solaris, AIX SGI Irix, IBMi Series 400, IBM S/390 HP-UX IBM
		Sun Web Server, WebSphere, Netscape Enterprise Server, GemStone, IBM WebSphere, Zeus, Lotus Domino	OS/2 SCO UnixWare Apple Mac OS X
		WebStar	
Apache::ASP	Apache-ASP.org	Apache	Linux, Unix, Windows

Some Examples

Now that you've seen the requirements for using Active Server Pages, let's start examining a few basic examples. The first example uses a server-side VBScript to display a message in the browser window.

When you are creating an Active Server Page, the server-side script can be identified in one of the following two ways:

- Use the server-side script block identifiers "<%" and "%>".

- Use the <SCRIPT> tag with the RUNAT="SERVER" attribute.

Functionally, both of these give you the same result, but it's important to note that the latter is the only one allowed in ASP.NET (discussed in a later chapter). Using either of these methods, you can mix your script blocks with static HTML tags. Since chapter 1 covered HTML, I won't spend a lot of time on HTML tags here, except to review those tags that are pertinent to the examples shown.

The sample ASP code shown in Figure 2.2 will display the current time in the browser window. To try this example, enter the code and save the file to the default directory of your Web server (for example, "C:\Inetpub\wwwroot on IIS"). Assuming that this file were named "time.asp," you would access it from a Web browser by entering the following URL: *http://Webserver/time.asp*

```
<HTML>
<HEAD>
<TITLE>Sample ASP Clock</TITLE>
</HEAD>
<BODY BGCOLOR="BLACK">
<FONT COLOR="GREEN">
<SCRIPT LANGUAGE="VBScript" RUNAT="SERVER">
RESPONSE.WRITE NOW()
</SCRIPT>
</BODY>
</HTML>
```

Figure 2.2: This Active Server Page displays the current time and date.

When this page is loaded into your browser, right-click it and select "View Source." The HTML shown in Figure 2.3 should be displayed. Notice that the script block is not visible to the user.

```
<HTML>
<HEAD>
<TITLE>Sample ASP Clock</TITLE>
</HEAD>
<BODY BGCOLOR="BLACK">
<FONT COLOR="GREEN">
03/01/2003  11:31:04
</BODY>
</HTML>
```

Figure 2.3: The viewable source does not include the script block.

ASP Objects

While the script portion of the previous example is pretty basic, it gives a good example of what Active Server Pages are all about. First, HTML defines the page title, background color, and font color. Then, the script code uses the Write method of the Response object to send output to the browser.

When writing ASP scripts, a special set of ASP objects are available within the VBScript language to assist in the programming process. These objects give you access to *application programming interfaces* (*APIs*) that allow you to manipulate the document displayed in the browser. Each of these objects has the following:

- *Properties* set or read information about the object.

- *Methods* execute an action on an object.

- *Collections* contain items related to the object.

The Response object will be used heavily throughout all of the examples in this book. This object allows you to control what is displayed in the browser. Table 2.2 shows all of the available properties, methods, and collections for the Response object.

Table 2.2: The Properties, Methods, and Collections of the Response Object

Name	Type	Values	Description
AddHeader	Method	N/A	Sets the value of a specified HTML header.
AppendToLog	Method	N/A	Adds a specified string to the end of the Web server log entry.
Buffer	Property	True/false	Defines whether or not to buffer content before sending it to the browser.
CacheControl	Property	Public/private	Defines whether or not page contents are cached on a proxy server.
Charset	Property	String value	Inserts a character-set name into the content-type header.
Clear	Method	N/A	Clears out the contents of the buffer.
ContentType	Property	MIME type	Defines the HTTP content type of data being sent to the browser.
Cookies	Collection	N/A	Used to set or read cookie values.
End	Method	N/A	Stops further script processing and sends buffer content to the browser.
Expires	Property	Numeric value	Define the length of time before a cached page expires. A value of zero disables caching of this page.
Expires Absolute	Property	Date/time	Defines the date and time when a cached page expires.
Flush	Method	N/A	Sends the contents of the buffer to the browser and clears it.
IsClient Connected	Property	True/false	Identifies whether or not the client is connected to the server.
Pics	Property	String value	Defines the PICS content rating.
Redirect	Method	N/A	Redirects control to a specified page. Only valid if no HTML headers have been sent to the browser.
Status	Property	String value	Contains the contents of the status line returned by the server.
Write	Method	N/A	Sends output to the browser.

36

Table 2.3: Objects Used within an Active Server Page

Object	Description
Application	Defines or reads variables that are specific to a Web application (a Web site counter, for example).
Request	Allows values to be retrieved from the client browser.
Response	Sends data to the browser window.
Server	Controls various attributes related to the Web server itself.
Session	Creates or reads values that are specific to a user's current session.

As you can see, the Response object controls output that is sent to the browser. For example, the Cookies collection, when used with the Response object, would define Cookie values that are stored on the client computer, to be retrieved by the application at a later time.

Active Server Pages have their own subset of objects used to control input from the client browser, output to the browser, and values used by the Web application. Table 2.3 contains a list of these objects and the functions they perform.

In the same way that the Response object writes information out, the Request object reads information in. One of the primary uses of Request is to read information sent into the Active Server Page. This is done using either the Querystring or Form collections. Each of these collections allows you to read "variables" from another Web page. The Querystring collection accesses variables supplied as part of the query string that is appended to the URL with a question mark:

http://myserver/myfirst.asp?fname=JOHN&lname=DOE

Query strings are generated automatically by an HTML form that uses the GET method, but they can also be manually inserted into a hyperlink. In the example link, the variables "fname" and "lname" are sent to the ASP specified. Notice that the ampersand character separates the query string variables. To read these variables into the ASP, you would use the following two lines of VBScript:

```
FirstName=REQUEST.QUERYSTRING("fname")
LastName=REQUEST.QUERSTRING("lname")
```

The one downside to using the Querystring collection is that the variable names and values can be seen within the URL on the browser. This can be a problem if you need to supply information to your Active Server Page that you don't want the user to see. This problem can be avoided by using the Form collection.

Like Querystring, values for the Form collection can be passed automatically from an HTML form. The difference is that the HTML <FORM> tag must use the POST method rather than the GET method. When the HTML form is submitted, any objects within the form will be passed through the Form collection. The Form variables are read using the same method as Querystring variables. Form variables, however cannot be appended to the URL as Querystring variables can.

In some cases, you won't always know the names of the Querystring or Form variables. To allow for this, you can use the For Each..Next loop. This loop is similar to a standard For.Next loop, with a few exceptions. A regular For.Next loop bases its looping on a starting value and an ending value. The resulting Numeric field is incremented based on the Step value provided. The For Each..Next loop feeds the name of each Item within the specified Collection into the supplied variable.

Here is an example of how to read all Form variables using a For Each..Next loop:

```
<%
For Each var In Request.Form
    Response.Write var & " = " & Request.Form (var)
Next
%>
```

In this example, each Form variable and its value will be displayed in the Web browser.

The Request object can do much more than just pass values between Web pages. Table 2.4 contains a list of the properties, methods, and collections available for the Request object.

Variable data within any of the five collections in the table can be retrieved simply by specifying *Request("variablename")*. When this form of the Request object is used, the application will search through each of these collections to find the matching variable. Since searching through each of the collections can be time-consuming, the preferred method is to retrieve data through the specific collection name. There are circumstances, however, when you might want to use this functionality. For example, your application might sometimes supply variable data through the Querystring collection, and other times use the Form collection. Using the search feature, your application could simply access the variable using the *Request("variablename")* form, so it wouldn't have to deal with figuring out which collection was used.

The Server Variables collection contains information specific to your server and the client connected to it. For example, the command below would retrieve the authorized user name of the user requesting the Web page:

Table 2.4: The Properties, Methods, and Collections of the Request Object

Name	Type	Description
Binary Read	Method	Retrieves a specified number of bytes of data supplied by the POST method into a safe array.
ClientCertificate	Collection	Retrieves the value of variables in the client certificate that is sent in the request.
Cookie	Collection	Reads the value of cookies.
Form	Collection	Reads the value of Form variables.
Querystring	Collection	Contains all variables supplied to the page through the query string.
ServerVariable	Collection	Reads attributes of the Web server or the client browser.
TotalBytes	Property	Defines the total number of data bytes sent by the client request; read-only.

```
User=Request.ServerVariable("AUTH_USER")
```

In this case, the AUTH_USER server variable is used to obtain the desired information. This specific variable will only return a value if your Web site requires a user name and password. If the Web site allows anonymous access, this variable will return an empty string. A list of some of the available ServerVariable items can be found in Table 2.5.

These values can be used to control the flow of your application in many ways. For example, you could use information from the HTTP_USER_AGENT variable to determine that a client request came from a PDA running Microsoft Pocket PC, and then redirect to a page specifically formatted for that device. The ASP code shown below would accomplish this, using the Response.Redirect method:

```
<%
UserAgent = Request.ServerVariables("HTTP_USER_AGENT")
IsPocketPC = (InStr(UserAgent, "Windows CE") > 0)

If IsPocketPC Then
    Response.Redirect("pda.asp")
Else
    Response.Redirect("default.asp")
End If
%>
```

This example first places the value of the HTTP_USER_AGENT server variable into the program variable UserAgent. Next, the InStr function looks for the string "Windows CE" within the UserAgent variable. If there is a match, the value of IsPocketPC will be TRUE; otherwise, it will be false. Finally, this value is used with an IF..THEN statement to redirect the browser to the appropriate page for the device.

The Session and Application objects perform similar functions. These objects allow you to define variables that will be available to multiple pages within your application, without having to be passed through the Querystring or Form collections. To set or read a Session variable, you reference the variable as you

Table 2.5: Commonly Used ServerVariable Items

Variable Name	Description
ALL_HTTP	Retrieves all of the HTTP headers from the client.
APPL_PHYSICAL_PATH	Retrieves the physical path corresponding to the metabase path returned in APPL_MD_PATH. The metabase is the database used internally by IIS to store Web server settings.
AUTH_PASSWORD	Returns the user password if basic authentication is used.
AUTH_TYPE	Returns the authentication method used to validate users when they attempt to access a protected script.
AUTH_USER	Supplies the user name sent in the client's authorization header.
HTTP_HOST	Contains the host name of the Web server.
HTTP_USER_AGENT	Returns a string containing information about the client. This string can be used to determine the operating system and browser on the client.
HTTPS	Indicates whether the request came on a secure port.
LOCAL_ADDR	Identifies the IP address on which a request came in.
LOGON_USER	Returns the Windows account used to access the page.
REMOTE_ADDR	Returns the IP address of the client.
REMOTE_HOST	Identifies the name of the client system.
REQUEST_METHOD	Determines the method used to send data to the server (GET or POST).
SERVER_NAME	Provides the Web server's host name.
SERVER_PORT	Returns the TCP/IP port on which a request came in.
SERVER_SOFTWARE	Returns name and version information for the Web server software.
URL	Returns the base portion of the URL page.

would any item within a collection. The statement below would read the value of the Session variable "customer" into the field Cust:

```
CUST = SESSION("customer")
```

Session variables exist until the user ends the current session with the Web server, or until Session.Abandon is executed. This method removes any session variables for the current session. In addition to the Abandon method, the Session object supports two properties, SessionID and Timeout. The SessionID property contains a unique numeric identifier for the current session. The Timeout property specifies a timeout value for the current session.

You would use the Session object in the same way as the LDA or QTEMP from within an application on the iSeries. Just like the LDA, Session variables are only available to the session running the application. Like objects stored in QTEMP, objects created using the Session object no longer exist when the session is closed.

The Application object exists from the time the Web application is created. A Web application is defined as a set of Web pages under a common root folder. Application variables are cleared when the Web server is restarted. Application variables are defined by the same method as Session variables. The line below shows how an Application variable would be defined:

```
Counter=Application("Counter")
```

The value of the Application variable is available to all Sessions running on the Web server. For this reason, Application variables are an ideal way to create a page counter. You use Application objects in the same way that you use data areas on the iSeries. These variables can be used to store values and share them between applications.

The Server object is used to access methods and properties of the Web server. This object performs several functions, not the least of which is to provide access to an ActiveX control on the server. Table 2.4 lists the properties and methods of the Server object.

The ASPError object is used in conjunction with the Server.GetLastError method. This object retrieves information about the most recent ASP error that has occurred. This object supports the properties listed in Table 2.5.

Table 2.4: The Properties and Methods of the Server ASP Object

Name	Type	Description
ScriptTimeout	Property	Defines the amount of time the ASP script runs before a timeout occurs.
CreateObject	Method	Creates a server-side ActiveX control.
Execute	Method	Calls another ASP page as though it were part of this page.
GetLastError	Method	Builds an ASPError object containing details of the most recent error.
HTMLEncode	Method	Replaces any special characters in a specified string with their HTML-encoded equivalents.
MapPath	Method	Returns the physical disk path for the provided virtual path.
Transfer	Method	Transfers control to a specified ASP page while leaving any ASP objects intact.
URLEncode	Method	Encodes a specified URL in the same way that HTMLEncode encodes a text string.

Table 2.5: The Properties of the ASPError Object

Property	Description
ASPCode	Returns the ASP error code related to the error.
Number	Results in the numeric error code returned by a COM component.
Source	Supplies the actual source code for the line in error.
Category	Provides a string value identifying what generated the error (IIS, a COM component, or a scripting language).
File	Contains the name of the ASP file where the error originated.
Line	Returns the line number in error.
Column	Identifies the column position of the error within the error line.
Description	Contains a short text description of the error.
ASPDescription	For ASP errors, provides a longer description of the error.

To access the ASPError object, you first need to define the relationship to the Server object, as shown here:

```
Set objASPError = Server.GetLastError
```

In this example, all of the ASPError object properties are now available to the object objASPError. This object can be used to create custom error-trapping for your application. All errors that are generated access a default Web page on IIS named "500-100.asp." This file can be overridden to a specified custom ASP file that uses the ASPError object. To override, follow these steps:

1. From the IIS Administrator, right-click on your Web site.

2. Select Properties, then select Customer Errors, and look for 500;100.

3. Click Properties, then click Select URL.

4. Enter the URL for the modified version of the "500-100.asp" page.

Within this modified page, you might choose to write error entries to a database file that contains an error log. You might also send an e-mail message to an administrator to notify him or her that an error has occurred with the application. You'll see how to accomplish each of these a little later on.

The final ASP object that we'll examine here is the ObjectContext object. ObjectContext allows you to create transactional ASP scripts. Creating ASP scripts that use transaction processing allows you to commit or abort a group of transactions performed on an object in a single step. You would use ObjectContext in the same way that SQL uses transaction processing. This is also similar to using commitment control in an iSeries application.

ObjectContext has only two methods. The ObjectContext.SetComplete method finalizes all transactions performed within the script, while ObjectContext.Abort cancels any transactions performed within the script. For transaction processing to be active, the script must contain the @TRANSACTION directive as its first line, as shown here:

```
<@TRANSACTION value>
```

The value specified is used to define whether or not transaction processing will be used. A value of either REQUIRED or REQUIRED_NEW will cause a transaction to be initiated. If values of SUPPORTED or NOT_SUPPORTED are used, a transaction will not be initiated. One transaction can span multiple ASP pages if control is transferred through the use of the Server.Transfer or Server.Execute method. In either of these cases, if REQUIRED is specified on the @TRANSACTION directive, the new page will continue within the transaction of the original ASP script. If the original script did not use transaction processing, the new script will create a new transaction.
The code snippet in Figure 2.4 shows an example of how ObjectContext is used.

```
< @TRANSACTION REQUIRED >
```

In this example, the SetComplete method is used. This is not necessary, however, since the transaction will automatically be set complete upon completion of the script.

```
<HTML>
<BODY>
<SCRIPT LANGUAGE="VBScript" RUNAT="SERVER">
Set objMine=Server.CreateObject("MyObj.Name")
If objMine.Value=0 Then
    ObjectContext.SetAbort
Else
    ObjectContext.SetComplete
End If
</SCRIPT>
</BODY>
</HTML>
```

Figure 2.4: This script uses ObjectContext for transaction processing.

Using HTML Forms with ASP

Now that you've seen each of the ASP objects, let's examine how to use these objects to create Web pages. ASP scripts work together with HTML in an Active Server Page in the same way that RPG works with a display file to create an interactive application on the iSeries. As you saw earlier, the Response.Write method can be used to send output to the browser. This output can include HTML tags, which means that your application can dynamically create the page.

To create input fields within Web pages, use HTML forms. The values entered into the HTML form are passed to the ASP script through the Request.Querystring and Request.Form collections. Figure 2.5 contains code for a simple HTML form.

This sample first uses the <FORM> tag to define form information. The NAME attribute identifies the form, while the METHOD attribute defines how the values from the form will be passed. A method of POST sends the variables through the Request.Form collection. The GET method will send the values through the Request.Querystring collection.

Next, in addition to some simple headings, each of the input fields is defined. Again, the NAME property is used to identify the variable within the Request.Querystring or Request.Form collection. The TYPE property defines the type of input field being created. All of the fields here are simple text boxes. The SIZE property defines the size of the text box as a number of characters. The

```
<html>
<body>
<form name="sampleform" method="POST" action="process.asp" ID="Form1">
Name: <input type="TEXT" name="Name" size =35 ID=""text"1"><br>
Address:<input type="TEXT" name="Addr1" size=35 ID=""text"2"><br>
City, St ,Zip: <input type="TEXT" name="City" size=15 ID=""text"3"> 
<input type="TEXT" name="State" size=2 maxlength="2" ID=""text"4"> 
<input type="TEXT" name="Zip" size=5 maxlength="5" ID=""text"5"><br>
<input type="SUBMIT" value="Process" ID=""submit1" NAME="submit1">
</form>
</body>
</html>
```

Figure 2.5: This HTML code creates an input form.

MAXLENGTH property used on some of the fields defines a maximum accepted length for the variable.

The final field used within the form is also an input field, but this time it is defined as SUBMIT, which creates an input button that can be used to send the form to the server. The NAME parameter is used once again to identify this item when the form is submitted. The VALUE property, in this case, serves two purposes. First, it provides the text that will be displayed on the button. Second, it is the value used for the SUBMIT button when the form is submitted.

Using a text editor, enter the code in Figure 2.5 and save it with the name "sample.html." Now, open the file in your Web browser by typing the full path to the file, including the file name, in the address bar. You should see something similar to Figure 2.6.

At this point, you might be wondering where the ASP code comes in. Notice that the ACTION parameter on the <FORM> tag defines a page called "process.asp." This is the Active Server Page that will process this form. Figure 2.7 contains the code for this page.

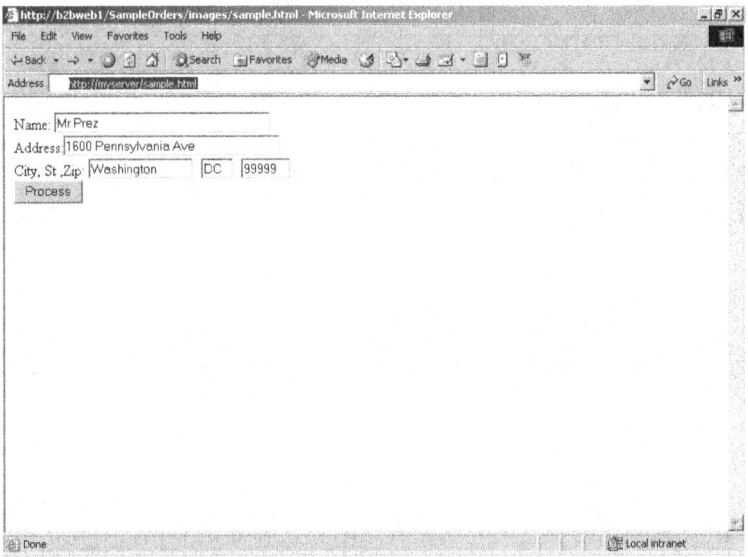

Figure 2.6: This is how the sample form in Figure 2.5 will look in the browser.

```
<html>
<body>
<script language="VBScript" runat="Server">
Dim var, val
For Each X in Request.Form
    var=X
    val=Request.Form(X)
    Response.Write var & " = " & val & "<br>"
Next
</script>
</body>
</html>
```

Figure 2.7: This ASP script displays the data from the form in Figure 2.6.

This example will take the values entered on the sample HTML form and display the variable names and their values in the browser window. The For Each..Next statement reads all of the values within the Request.Form collection. The values are sent out to the browser window using the Response.Write method. Notice that the HTML tag <BR> inserts a line break at the end of each line. This is a perfect example of how to combine variable values with HTML tags to create dynamic output. Figure 2.8 shows how the formatted output will appear in the browser window.

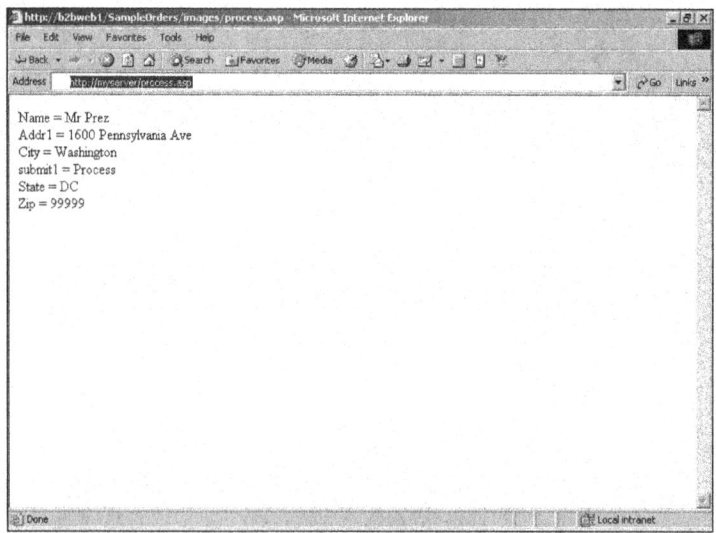

Figure 2.8: This is the ASP output from the script in Figure 2.7.

To take this example a little further, you can use an Active Server Page to create the HTML form. This gives you the ability to include or exclude form items dynamically. The example in Figure 2.9 creates values in a list box using a For..Next loop.

In this example, the <SELECT> tag creates a list box. The <OPTION> tags that provide the content for the list box are created by ASP code. The text between <OPTION> and </OPTION> defines what will be displayed for each option's value. This would allow you, for example, to display state names within a list, but return the state abbreviation to your ACTION page. Figure 2.10 shows what the output for this page would look like in a browser window. Using the same "process.asp" page created earlier, the value selected will be displayed in the browser window.

In both of these examples, the <INPUT> tag with TYPE of "SUBMIT" is used to create a command button to send the screen back to the server for processing. It's pretty easy to draw a correlation between this button and a function key within a display file on the iSeries. When you also consider that it's possible to have multiple submit buttons within the same form, it's even easier to see how similar these buttons are to function keys.

```
<html>
<body>
Select a range of values:
<form name="sampleform" method="POST" action="process.asp">
<select name="listvalue">
<script language="VBScript" runat="Server">
For I = 0 to 150000 step 15000
    J=I+14999
    Response.Write "<option value='" & I & "'>" & I & " - " & _
    J & "</option>"
Next
</script>
</select>
<input type=SUBMIT value="Submit Page">
</form>
</body>
</html>
```

Figure 2.9: This HTML code creates an input form.

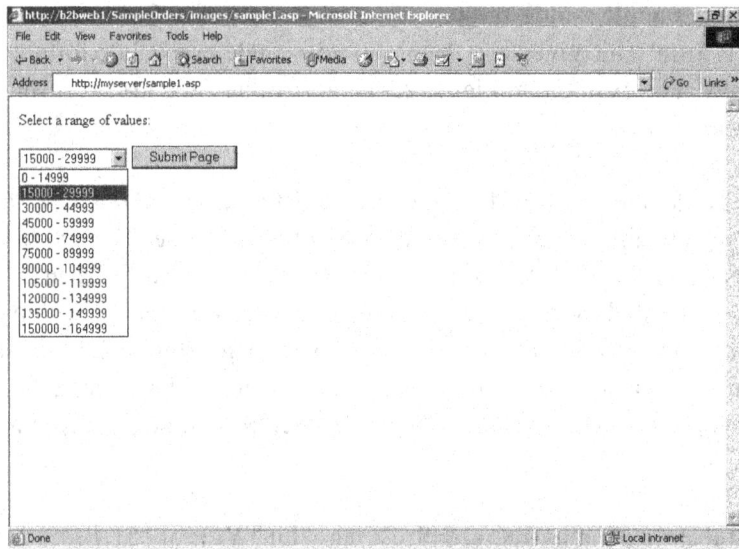

Figure 2.10: The options in this list box are created by an ASP page.

The example in Figure 2.11 takes this idea even further, by creating an HTML form that displays three "functions" along the bottom of the form. The value returned into the input field named "Function" determines how the page defined on the form's ACTION parameter should proceed. This is done similarly to the way an RPG program might deal with function keys.

```
<html>
<body>
<form name="sampleform" method="POST" action="process2.asp">
Name:<input type="TEXT" name="Name" size =35><br>
Address:<input type="TEXT" name="Addr1" size=35><br>
City, St, Zip:<input type="TEXT" name="City" size=15> 
<input type="TEXT" name="State" size=2 maxlength="2"> 
<input type="TEXT" name="Zip" size=5 maxlength="5"><br>
<input type="SUBMIT" name="function" value="Update">
<input type="SUBMIT" name="function" value="Cancel">
<input type="SUBMIT" name="function" value="Display">
</form>
</body>
</html>
```

Figure 2.11: This sample uses command buttons in place of function keys.

The ASP code for "process2.asp" is shown in Figure 2.12. This sample first reads the value of the Function variable, which contains the defined value for the SUBMIT button. Next, the Select Case statement controls the program flow based on each of the possible "function key" values. The basic program logic used in Figure 2.11 is very similar to how you would accomplish the same task in an RPG program.

In addition to simple text fields and command buttons, you can also create radio buttons and check boxes, and send their values through the Form or Querystring collections. Radio buttons are created by using the <INPUT> tag with

```
<!-- include functions.asp -->
<html>
<body>
<script language="VBScript" runat="Server">
Dim Fnc

' Read "function" variable from the FORM collection
Fnc=Request.Form("function")

' Use SELECT CASE to control the application flow
Select Case Fnc
    ' Call Update Routine
      Case "Update"
          Call Update()
    ' Redisplay main screen
      Case "Cancel"
          Response.Redirect "default.html"
    ' Display Form collection
      Case "Display"
          For Each x In Request.Form
              VarName=x
              VarVal=Request.Form(x)
          If VarName<>"function" Then
              Response.Write VarName * " = " & VarVal
          End If
          Next
End Select
</script>
</body>
</html>
```

Figure 2.12: This sample uses command buttons in place of function keys.

51

TYPE="RADIO." Radio buttons are normally used for multiple-choice selections. You define multiple radio buttons as one group by giving them the same name, as shown in Figure 2.13.

When this example is loaded into your browser, you'll see that by selecting one option, any other that is selected is unselected automatically. When the page is submitted, the value of the variable "Send" will reflect the option that was highlighted. Use a check box, on the other hand, when you want to allow an option to be defined as "on" or "off." If you were to change the TYPE on the example in Figure 2.13 from RADIO to CHECKBOX, it would be possible to check all three options at the same time. When the page was submitted, all three values would be returned into the Form collection. Table 2.6 contains a complete list of the Form objects available.

While ASP isn't a requirement to use HTML forms, HTML forms are a key part of Active Server Pages. This is because you use HTML forms to pass values to the ASP scripts. There are times, however, when you'll want to do some type of validation prior to sending the form back to the server. For this, you can use *client-side scripts.*

Client VBScripting and JavaScripting

In addition to creating scripts that run on the server, you can also create scripts in VBScript or JavaScript that run within the client browser. This ability is

```
<html>
<body>
<form name="sendto" method="POST" action="report.asp" ID="Form1">
Send Report To:<br><input type="RADIO" name="send"
value='P'>Printer</input><br>
<input type="RADIO" name="send" value='F'>File</input><br>
<input type="RADIO" name="send" value='S'>Screen</input><br>
<input type="SUBMIT" value="Process" ID=""submit1" NAME="submit1">
</form>
</body>
</html>
```

Figure 2.13: Radio buttons are created using the <INPUT> tag, as shown here.

Table 2.6: Objects That Can Be Used within an HTML Form

HTML Tag	Description
<INPUT TYPE="BUTTON">	Displays a command button on the form. This type of button does not automatically cause any action on the form.
<INPUT TYPE="CHECKBOX">	Appears on the form as a check box.
<INPUT TYPE="IMAGE">	Displays a specified image file on the form that will submit the form when clicked.
<INPUT TYPE="PASSWORD">	Displays a text box in which all entered characters appear as asterisks. This type is used for password entry.
<INPUT TYPE="RADIO">	Displays a radio button within the form.
<INPUT TYPE="RESET">	Appears as a command button, but will reset all of the values on the form to their defaults.
<INPUT TYPE="SUBMIT">	Displays a command button on the form that will automatically submit the form to the server.
<INPUT TYPE="TEXT">	Provides a single-line text box within the form.
<SELECT> <OPTION>	Act together to create a list box on the form. The SELECT tag defines the list box itself. The OPTION tag defines each of the items within the list box.
<TEXTAREA>	Similar to the TEXT type, but allows multiple lines of text to be entered into one field.

a double-edged sword, however. It does allow you to read the contents of a form prior to sending it to the server. At the same time, client scripts must be written in a way that allow for maximum compatibility. Different browsers might support different levels of client scripting. It's also entirely possible that a client might not have client scripts enabled at all. In any case, the following examples provide an introduction to client-script techniques.

Handling Mouse Events

Many of the objects within a Web page have events that can have client-scripting functions assigned to them. For example, a cell within an HTML table has ONMOUSEOVER and ONMOUSEOUT events. These two events are fired when the pointer is moved over or off of the cell, respectively. You can use these events to change the appearance of the cell when the user moves the pointer over it.

The Web page in Figure 2.14 uses a client script to highlight the text when the mouse pointer is placed over each of the cells. This example creates three cells within a table, and highlights each cell as the mouse pointer moves over it.

```html
<html>
<title>Mouse Over Client Script Example</title>
<body>
<table border=1>
    <tr>
        <td onmouseover='mouseover()' onmouseout='mouseout()'>
            Cell 1
        </td>
        <td onmouseover='mouseover()' onmouseout='mouseout()'>
            Cell 2
        </td>
        <td onmouseover='mouseover()' onmouseout='mouseout()'>
            Cell 3
        </td>
    </tr>
</table>
</body>
<script language='JavaScript'>
function mouseover(){
 var srcElement;
 srcElement=window.event.srcElement;
 srcElement.style.color= "White";
 srcElement.bgColor = "Black";
}

function mouseout(){
 var srcElement;
 srcElement=window.event.srcElement;
 srcElement.style.color= "Black";
 srcElement.bgColor = "White";
}
</script>
</html>
```

Figure 2.14: This sample assigns a client-side JavaScript to an event.

In this example, you determine the cell that is highlighted by using the Window.Event.srcElement object. The Window object is used to read and set attributes of the browser window or items within the browser window (in this case, the cells). After assigning the Window.Event.srcElement object to a variable named srcElement, you can redefine properties of the cell. In this case, the code changes the background color using the bgColor property, and changes the font color using the Style.Color property.

Figure 2.15 shows what this code would look like in a browser. In the browser, the cell coloring would change when the mouse pointer hovered over it. The coloring would return to normal when the ONMOUSEOUT event fired for the cell.

Client-side Form Validation

You can use this same technique to validate an entry in a form prior to submitting the form to the server. This is done by creating a function for use with the form's ONSUBMIT event. This event is fired when the form is submitted

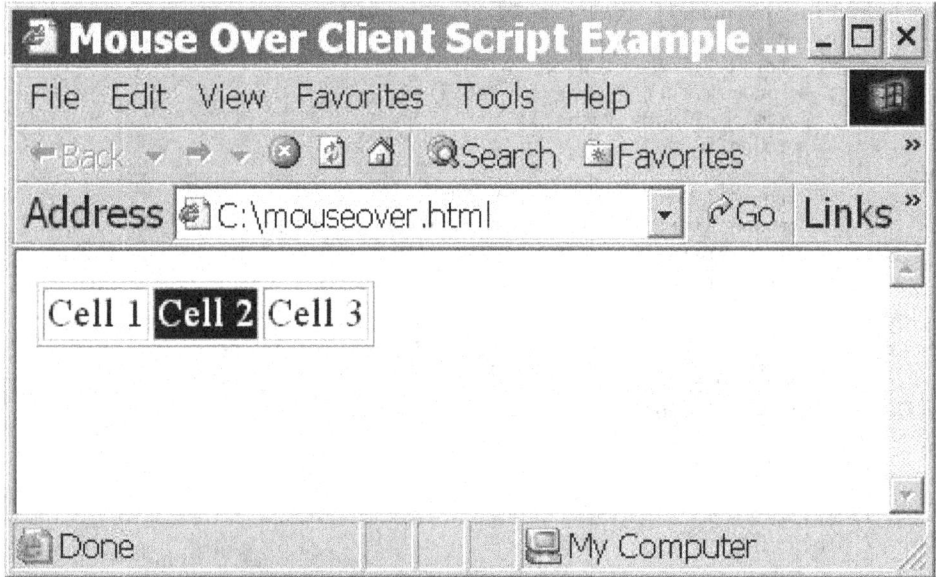

Figure 2.15: The "Mouseover" example as it appears in the browser.

through the use of a SUBMIT button or image. This technique can be used for basic data validation, like checking for the length of data entered into a field or verifying that a given field has an entry. The example shown in Figure 2.16 uses a client-side Java Script to validate three different form fields.

Each of the fields in Figure 2.16 has its own validation check. The Name field is simply checked to ensure that a value was entered. This is done through the use of a JavaScript "If" statement.

```
<html>
<body>
<form name="form1" method="POST" action="p2.asp"
onsubmit="return validate();">
* = Required Field<br>
Name *: <input type="TEXT" name="FullName" size =35 ID="FullName"><br>
E-Mail:<input type="TEXT" name="EMail" size=35 ID="EMail"><br>
Phone #:<input type="TEXT" name="Phone" size=15 ID="Phone"><br>
<input type="SUBMIT" value="Submit" ID="submit1" NAME="submit1">
</form>
</body>
<script language="JavaScript">
function validate() {
    if (form1.FullName.value == '') {
        window.alert('A Name is Required');
        form1.FullName.focus();
        return(false);
    }
    if (form1.EMail.value.search('@')==-1) {
        window.alert('E-mail address is invalid');
        form1.EMail.focus();
        return(false);
    }
    if (form1.Phone.value.length<10) {
        window.alert("Phone number is invalid");
        form1.Phone.focus();
        return(false);
    }
    return true;
}
</script>
</html>
```

Figure 2.16: This example uses a client-side script for data validation.

56

In JavaScript, all grouped statements (If, For, etc.), along with functions themselves, are grouped using the { and } bracket characters. For functions, this is done using the following format:

```
function  functioname() {
'  function code
}
```

Rather than require an End Function statement as would be used in a VBScript, you simply use the close bracket. An If statement is defined in a similar manner:

```
if (condition) {
'   conditional code
}
```

This example shows that the If statement is followed immediately by the condition enclosed in parentheses, and then the conditional code enclosed in brackets. Each of the fields within a form is referenced as shown here:

```
formname.fieldname.value
```

In this example *formname* corresponds to the name of an HTML form. *Fieldname* references the input field within that form. The *value* property retrieves the value of the field.

To get back to the example in Figure 2.16, the first If statement simply checks to see whether FullName is blank. If this field is blank, a message box signifying the error will be displayed using the Window.Alert command. Next, the Focus() method is used on the FullName field in the same way that a Position Cursor Display Attribute [DSPATR(PC)] would be used in a display file on the iSeries. It will cause the cursor to be placed in the FullName field. Then, the return(False); command is used. This will cause the HTML form to be redisplayed, after displaying the message box.

The Email field's address validation is slightly more complex. For this field, the script not only ensures that the field not contain a value, but specifically that it contains the @ character. This is done by using the Search JavaScript function. This function scans the string on which it is used for the specified string value. If the value is not found, a message box is displayed, notifying the user of the error. As with the FullName, the Focus() function positions the cursor to this field when the form is redisplayed by returning the False value.

The third validation is on the Phone field. This validation checks to ensure that the value in this field is no less than 10 positions. If the value is less than 10 positions, the same logic used for the other fields is used to display a message box and redisplay the form, with the cursor positioned at this field. Figure 2.17 shows an example of what the output from this sample page will look like.

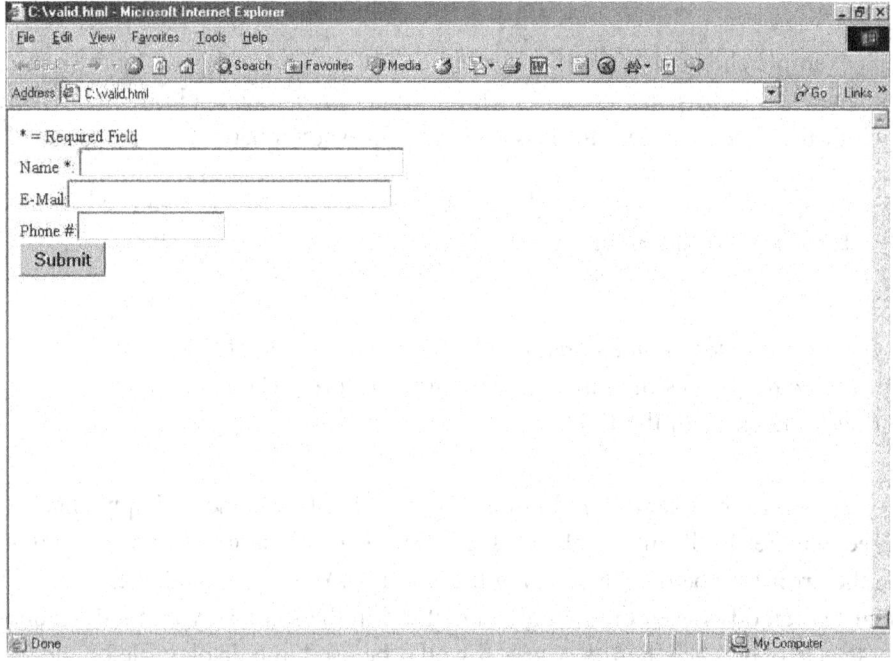

Figure 2.17: Each of these fields is validated using a client-side JavaScript.

VBScript Versus JavaScript

The two examples you just looked at both use JavaScript code running on the client. For these examples to work properly, the browser must support JavaScript. Another option for client-side scripting is to use the Visual Basic scripting language. This is basically the sample scripting language you use with server-side scripting, minus any of the ASP objects. The code in Figure 2.18 contains a sample client VBScript.

This example is basically a duplicate of Figure 2.14, with one exception: the JavaScript code has been replaced with its VBScript equivalent. The similarities

```html
<html>
<title>Mouse Over Client VBScript Example</title>
<body>
<table border=1>
   <tr>
      <td onmouseover='mouseover' onmouseout='mouseout'
      language=VBScript> Cell 1 </td>
      <td onmouseover='mouseover' onmouseout='mouseout'
      language=VBScript> Cell 2 </td>
      <td onmouseover='mouseover' onmouseout='mouseout'
      language=VBScript> Cell 3 </td>
   </tr>
</table>
</body>
<script language='VBScript'>
sub mouseover()
 Dim obj
 Set obj=window.event.srcElement
 obj.style.color="Red"
 obj.bgColor="Black"
end sub

sub mouseout()
 Dim obj
 Set obj=window.event.srcElement
 obj.style.color="Black"
 obj.bgColor="White"
end sub
</script>
</html>
```

Figure 2.18: This example uses a VBScript version of the Mouseover and Mouseout events.

include the use of the window.event.srcElement object. The differences including the use of the Dim statement in place of the Var statement to define variables. Functionally, this example is identical to Figure 2.14.

The decision to use either JavaScript or VBScript involves several factors, including your comfort level with each of these languages. In the end, however, the deciding factor might be browser compatibility. As a general rule, JavaScript is supported by more browsers that VBScript, so in my opinion JavaScript would be the client-side language of choice.

Summary

As you've seen in this chapter, ASP scripts allow you to dynamically adjust the HTML within a Web page. The ability to execute scripts on the Web server lets you control the output sent to the browser, while keeping these scripts "hidden" from the end user. In chapter 3, we'll take this to the next level by examining how to access data stored in the iSeries (or any other database) from within an ASP.

3

ASP Data Access

In chapter 2, you learned what Active Server Pages are and how they work. This chapter shows how to use an Active Server Page to access data within an external database. While the focus here is on accessing data in a DB2 database on the iSeries, the techniques discussed can be used to access any data source that's OLE DB or ODBC compliant.

Configuring Data Access

As mentioned in chapter 2, one of the great things about using a server-side script to access a database is that all of the data-access configuration is done on the server. Another advantage to this can be licensing, if you are accessing a database server that requires each client to have a client-access license (SQL Server, for example). In the case of an Active Server Page, the Web server is the only database client. The user accesses the page through the browser, and the Web server accesses the database.

In the case of the iSeries, you can use either ODBC or OLE DB to access the data. Both of these options are included with Client Access Express. The important thing is to ensure that you select both of these options when installing Client Access Express on your Web server. To do this, select "Custom" from the setup menu and expand the Data Access branch of the tree. Then, check both "ODBC" and "OLE DB Provider," as shown in Figure 3.1. Once this setup is complete, you're ready to go.

Components	Size	License Required
☑ Express Required Programs	0 K	
⊞ ☑ Express Optional Components	0 K	
⊞ ☑ AS/400 Operations Navigator	0 K	
⊟ ☑ Data Access	0 K	
⊞ ☑ Data Transfer	0 K	✔
☑ ODBC	0 K	
☑ OLE DB Provider	0 K	
☑ AFP Workbench Viewer	0 K	
☑ AS/400 Java Toolbox	0 K	
⊞ ☑ 5250 Display and Printer Emulator	0 K	✔

Figure 3.1: Select "ODBC" and "OLE DB Provider" from the Client Access Express setup.

ActiveX Data Objects

With the components in place, you're ready to start building data-access Web pages. You access the data source from your Active Server Page through *ActiveX Data Objects* (*ADO*). ADO can be used with either an ODBC data source or an OLE DB provider. Think of ADO as the telephone and ODBC or OLE DB as the phone line. That is, ADO is the tool that allows you to get to the data, and ODBC and OLE DB are the means by which ADO gets to that data.

ADO lets you access a database from an Active Server Page using standard SQL statements. Accessing a database using ADO involves the following four objects:

- *ADO Connection* defines information related to your data source, such as the system name and provider name, in addition to the user name and password.

- *ADO Command* is primarily used to run commands or perform "action" queries (such as update and delete) on the database. It can also define a data set for use with a Recordset object.

- *ADO Recordset* accesses data within a database.

- *ADO Error* is an object, or more correctly a collection, that identifies error information related to the ADO connection.

ADO Connection Object

The ADO Connection object is the highest-level piece to accessing the data source. The Connection object defines what type of data source you are accessing, how you get to the data source, and any security credentials required to access the data source. To create a new ADO Connection object within an ASP script, you would use code similar to the following:

```
<%
    Set conn=Server.CreateObject("ADODB.Connection")
    conn.ConnectionString="Provider=IBMDA400; Data Source=S1234567; " & _
    "User ID=user; Password=secret"
    conn.Open
%>
```

The first line in this example uses the CreateObject method of the Server object to create the ADO Connection object. The next statement defines the ConnectionString property of the new Connection object. The connection string allows you to define parameters related to the connection, such as the user name, OLE DB provider, and data source, as listed in Table 3.1. This example uses the IBM OLE DB provider for the iSeries. Finally, the Open method is executed on the Connection object to initiate a link to the defined ADO connection.

The provider can be defined on its own using the Provider property, as shown below:

```
<%
    Set conn=Server.CreateObject("ADODB.Connection")
    conn.Provider="IBMDA400"
    conn.ConnectionString="Data Source=192.168.0.5; User ID=user; " & _
                          "password=secret;"
    conn.Open
%>
```

Table 3.1: Some Parameters That Can Be Defined on ConnectionString

Parameter	Description
Provider	Defines the OLE DB provider to be used. IBM's OLE DB provider for the iSeries is IBMDA400.
Data Source	Defines the name of the server for an OLE DB provider. This parameter can also be used to specify the file name for a file-based database like Microsoft Access.
User ID	Specifies the user name to be used when logging on to the database server.
Password	Specifies the password to be used when logging on to the database server.
Initial Catalog	For the SQL Server OLE DB provider, defines the default database to be accessed on the SQL Server. Not used for the iSeries OLE DB provider.
DNS	Can be used to define the name for an ODBC data source.

This example uses the Client Access OLE DB provider. Notice that it still defines the data source, user ID, and password attributes within the ConnectionString property.

To use an ODBC data source instead of the Client Access OLE DB provider to make an ADO connection, exclude the Provider property and modify the ConnectionString property, as shown here:

```
<%
  Set conn=Server.CreateObject("ADODB.Connection")
  conn.ConnectionString="DRIVER=Client Access ODBC Driver (32-bit); "&_
  "UID=USER;PWD=SECRET;SYSTEM=192.168.0.5"
  conn.Open
%>
```

In this example, the Driver attribute defines the ODBC driver to be used for the connection. The UID attribute supplies a user ID, and the PWD attribute identifies the password associated with the user ID. Finally, the System attribute provides the name or IP address of the data source.

Both the ConnectionString and Provider properties can be read and set at execution time. This means that not only can the value be set, but it can also be read back into your application. When reading the ConnectionString property, all of the available attributes will appear, not only those that you set when defining the property. For example, if you were to set the ConnectionString property from within an Active Server Page, and then display the value of ConnectionString back to the browser using Response.Write, you would see all of the connection attributes, not only those set when ConnectionString was initially defined. For a complete list of the collections, properties, and methods of the ADO Connection object, refer to Table 3.2.

Table 3.2: The Properties, Methods, and Collections of the ADO Connection Object

Item	Type	Description
Attributes	Property	Defines the transaction attributes of the Connection object.
Begin Trans	Method	Indicates the start of a new set of transactions for the Connection object.
Cancel	Method	Causes termination of the asynchronous method that was called most recently. This applies to an Execute or Open method.
Close	Method	Closes the Connection object.
Command Timeout	Property	Sets the amount of time a command is allowed to complete before it is cancelled.
CommitTrans	Method	Applies all transactions created since the most recent BeginTrans method call.
ConnectionString	Property	Allows the definition of attributes of the data source in one string.
ConnectionTimeout	Property	Defines the amount of time a connection is allowed to complete before a timeout occurs.
CursorLocation	Property	Indicates whether data cursors for this connection are held at the client or at the server.

Table 3.2: The Properties, Methods, and Collections of the ADO Connection Object, *continued*

Item	Type	Description
DefaultDatabase	Property	Defines the default database for the defined Connection object. In the case of SQL Server, this will be an SQL database. For the iSeries, this defines the default library name.
Errors	Collection	Retrieves error information for the Connection object.
IExecute	Method	Executes a command or creates a Recordset object without the use of a Command object.
IsolationLevel	Property	Used prior to the BeginTrans method to define the level of isolation for transaction processing.
Mode	Property	Defines the mode used to open the file (such as Read or Write), as well as the exclusivity with which the connection is opened.
Open	Method	Makes the initial connection to the data source defined on the Connection object.
OpenSchema	Method	Returns a Recordset object that contains information about the datasource defined on the Connection object.
Properties	Collection	Contains property objects that define attributes of the Connection object.
Provider	Property	Defines the OLE DB provider to be used for the connection. The IBM OLE DB provider for the iSeries will always be IBMDA400.
RollbackTrans	Method	Performs a rollback of all transactions created since the most recent BeginTrans method call.
State	Property	Returns the state of the defined Connection object as Closed, Opened, Connecting, Executing, or Fetching.
Version	Property	Returns a string that indicates the ADO version in use for this Connection object.

ADO Recordset Object

Once the ADO Connection object is defined, you're ready to use the Command or Recordset object. As described earlier, the Recordset object gives you access to the data within your database. Defining the Recordset object requires only a line of SQL code. The great thing about this is that you can define a Recordset that contains data from multiple files by using SQL's "JOIN" clause. This allows you to get the same effect that you would get on the iSeries by using an Open Query File.

The example in Figure 3.2 contains the source for an Active Server Page that displays the contents of the systables file on the iSeries. For future reference, this file contains information about all of the files in every library on your iSeries.

```
<!-- #include file="adovbs.inc" -->
<html><head></head>
<body>
File Listing
<table>
<%
    Set conn=Server.CreateObject("ADODB.Connection")
    conn.ConnectionString="DRIVER=Client Access ODBC Driver (32-bit); "&_
                          "UID=USER;PWD=SECRET;SYSTEM=192.168.0.5"
    conn.open
    Set rst=Server.CreateObject("ADODB.Recordset")
    rst.Open "SELECT * FROM QSYS2.SYSTABLES", conn, adOpenKeyset
    If Not rst.EOF
        Response.Write "<tr>"
        rst.MoveFirst
        For I=0 to rst.Fields.Count-1
            Response.Write "<th>" & rst.Fields(I).Name & "</th>"
        Next
        Response.Write "</tr>"

    Do Until rst.EOF
        Response.Write "<tr>"
        For I=0 to rst.Fields.Count-1
            Response.Write "<td>" & rst.Fields(I).Value & _
                          "</td>"
        Next
        Response.Write "</tr>"
        rst.MoveNext
```

Figure 3.2: This page displays a list of files using the ADO Recordset object (part 1 of 2).

```
    Loop
    End If
    rst.Close
    conn.Close
%>
</table>
</body>
</html>
```

Figure 3.2: This page displays a list of files using the ADO Recordset object (part 2 of 2).

The first line of code in Figure 3.2 uses the <!—INCLUDE> tag to incorporate constants that are defined in the Include file "Adovbs.inc." This file contains the VBScript definitions for the ADO constants used with the ADO objects. On a Windows PC, this file can be found in the folder "C:\Program Files\ Common Files\System\ado\."

After defining the Connection object as explained earlier, the code in Figure 3.2 creates a Recordset object using the Server.CreateObject method. The Open method of the Recordset object, along with the SQL statement, defines the data to be retrieved, followed by the ADO Connection object to be used as the ActiveConnection for the Recordset. The Fields collection of the Recordset object then retrieves attributes of the fields within the Recordset. The Count property of the Fields collection determines the number of fields within the Recordset.

Within the Fields collection, attributes of the individual fields can be retrieved in one of two ways:

- Use the numeric \value of the field's position within the Recordset, where zero is the first field, one is the second field, and so on.

- Specify a string value that contains the name of the field.

The Name property returns the field's name, while the Value property returns its value.

The first For..Next loop in Figure 3.2 writes the field names into the heading row of an HTML table, using <TH> tags. The second For..Next loop is contained within a Do loop, which is executed until the EOF condition occurs for the Recordset object. This second For..Next loop displays the values of each of the fields in the Recordset within the columns of an HTML table by writing <TD> and </TD> tags around each of the field names. The rows are created by writing <TR> and </TR> tags around the For..Next loop.

The MoveFirst and MoveNext methods of the Recordset object perform a similar function to the SETLL and READ op codes in RPG. As their names suggest, MoveFirst moves the cursor to the first record within the Recordset, and MoveNext moves the cursor to the next record. In a similar fashion, the MovePrev method can be used to move back one record within the Recordset. This method is similar to the RPG op code READP. Unlike these RPG op codes, however, records within an ADO Recordset are not selected or sorted using the key fields defined for the file. Instead, they are selected based on "WHERE" and "ORDER BY" SQL clauses specified on the Open method for the Recordset.

Table 3.3 lists the properties, methods, and collections of the Recordset object. Not all of the items listed in this table are available with all OLE DB providers. For example, the Client Access OLE DB provider does not support the PageCount, PageSize, and RecordCount properties. This can be a consideration if your application needs this type of information, so you will have to design your application with this in mind.

The third parameter of the Recordset's Open method defines the cursor type for the Recordset. It's important to use the correct cursor type for your application. Table 3.4 lists the available CursorType options and provides a brief description of how each is used.

When using a Forward Only or Static cursor, it's important to note that several ADO methods will not be available, including MoveFirst and MovePrev. If you attempted to use the MoveFirst method when accessing the iSeries OLE DB provider with a Static or Forward Only cursor, an end-of-file error would be returned on the Web server.

The default value for the CursorType parameter is Forward Only. If your application only requires that you read through a Recordset one time from beginning

Table 3.3: The Properties, Methods and Collections of the Recordset Object

Item	Type	Description
AbsolutePage	Property	Identifies the page containing the current record. The total record count is divided into pages as defined on the PageSize property.
AbsolutePosition	Property	Sets or returns the record position within the current Recordset.
ActiveCommand	Property	Returns the Command object that was used to create the Recordset.
ActiveConnection	Property	Sets or returns the Connection object associated with the Recordset.
BOF	Property	Returns True if the current record falls before the first record in the Recordset.
Bookmark	Property	Defines or retrieves a bookmark to the current record.
CacheSize	Property	Sets or retrieves a value identifying the number of records from the Recordset that are cached locally.
CursorLocation	Property	Defines or retrieves the type of cursor used with this Recordset (client or server).
CursorType	Property	Sets or retrieves the value that identifies the method with which the records are retrieved from the Recordset.
EOF	Property	Indicates that the last Read operation on the Recordset reached end-of-file.
Field	Collection	Describes data and value information for fields within a Recordset.
Filter	Property	Filters records within a Recordset. This property is specified as either a string, in the form of an SQL WHERE clause, or as an array containing bookmark objects that mark specific records within the Recordset.
Move	Method	Moves to a specified record number or bookmark within the provided Recordset.
MoveFirst	Method	Moves to the first record in a Recordset.

Table 3.3: The Properties, Methods and Collections of the Recordset
Object, *continued*

Item	Type	Description
MoveLast	Method	Moves to the last record in a Recordset.
MoveNext	Method	Reads the next record in a Recordset.
MovePrevious	Method	Reads the previous record in a Recordset.
Open	Method	Connects to a database and opens the defined Recordset object.
PageCount	Property	Identifies the number of record "pages" within the Recordset.
PageSize	Property	Identifies the number of records per page.
Properties	Collection	Provides access to attributes of a Recordset.
RecordCount	Property	Returns the number of records within the current Recordset.
Source	Property	Defines the source of the Recordset as either a Command object or an SQL statement.

to end, this cursor offers slightly better performance than the others. If, on the other hand, you need to move through your Recordset more randomly, the Dynamic or Keyset cursors would be the only choices. The Open method shown in Figure 3.2 uses the ADO constant adoOpenKeyset to indicate that the Recordset is to be opened using the Keyset cursor.

ADO Command Object

The Command object serves many purposes:

- Run an "action" query (such as update, delete, or insert) on a data source.

- Call a program on the iSeries.

- Execute an OS/400 command, through the use of the QCMDEXC API

Table 3.4: The Options for the CursorType parameter of the Recordset Object

Cursor Type	Numeric Value	Description
Forward Only	0	Allows you to read through your Recordset only once, and only in the forward direction.
Keyset	1	Allows you to read through the database in any direction. Records added by other users after the Recordset is created cannot be seen, but deleted records will become inaccessible.
Dynamic	2	Similar to a Keyset cursor, except that all updates or additions by other users will be visible within the Recordset object.
Static	3	Similar to Forward Only. Creates a static copy of the Recordset data that is used to search through the records. Additions, deletions, or updates by other users are not visible.

- Define the source for a Recordset, using a *parameterized* SQL statement. This type of SQL statement allows you to replace constant values with parameters that have their values set prior to opening the Recordset.

There are performance implications to using a parameterized query rather than simply rebuilding the SQL statement. A parameterized query will generally offer better performance, since the query optimizer will analyze the changed SQL source, but doesn't need to analyze the changed parameter values.

Figure 3.3 contains a sample ASP script that uses the ADO Command object to run an SQL "INSERT" statement. In this example, the Connection object is defined as in the earlier examples. Then, the source of the Command object is defined using the CommandText property. This property can contain either an SQL statement or a Call statement that can be used to execute a program the iSeries. The example here uses the "INSERT INTO" SQL statement to write a record into the defined file. This is analogous to an RPG WRITE operation.

After defining the CommandText property, the code in Figure 3.3 associates the ADO Connection object with the ADO Command object using the

```
<!-- #include file="adovbs.inc" -->
<html><head></head>
<body>
<%
   Set conn=Server.CreateObject("ADODB.Connection")
   conn.ConnectionString="Provider=IBMDA400; Data Source=S1234567; " & _
                         "User ID=user;Password=secret; "
   conn.open

   Set cmd=Server.CreateObject("ADODB.Command")
   cmd.CommandText="INSERT INTO mylib.myfile VALUES('ABC', 123) "
   cmd.ActiveConnection=conn
   cmd.Execute
   conn.Close
%>
</body>
</html>
```

Figure 3.3: This sample code executes an "action" query using an ADO Command object.

ActiveConnection property. Next, it calls the Execute method on the Command object. As its name indicates, the Execute method runs the command defined on the CommandText property. The final step is to close the Connection object. The Command object doesn't need to be closed because it is automatically closed when the Execute method is initiated.

The example shown in Figure 3.4 uses the Command object in a different way. This time, it calls a program on the iSeries. With the exception of the CommandText definition, this example uses the same sequence of events as in Figure 3.3.

```
<!-- #include file="adovbs.inc" -->
<html><head></head>
<body>
<%
   Set conn=Server.CreateObject("ADODB.Connection")
   conn.ConnectionString="Provider=IBMDA400; Data Source=S1234567; " & _
                         "User ID=user;Password=secret; "
```

Figure 3.4: This ASP example calls a program on the iSeries (part 1 of 2).

```
            conn.open
            Set cmd=Server.CreateObject("ADODB.Command")
            cmd.CommandText="CALL mylib.mypgm PARM('A', 'N') "
            cmd.ActiveConnection=conn
            cmd.Execute
            conn.Close
        %>
        </body>
        </html>
```

Figure 3.4: This ASP example calls a program on the iSeries (part 2 of 2).

The third example of using the ADO Command object is to define the source for a Recordset. This is done by setting the CommandText property to an SQL "SELECT" statement similar to those in Figure 3.2. One reason to use the Command object in this fashion is that it allows for the definition of parameters. Parameters can be used in place of static values within an SQL statement—in a "WHERE" clause, for example. When the query is run, the query optimizer will analyze the statement to optimize the access path. For example, consider the source below:

```
        <%
            Set conn=Server.CreateObject("ADODB.Connection")
            conn.ConnectionString="Provider=IBMDA400; Data Source=S1234567; " &_
                            "User ID=user;Password=secret; "
            conn.open
            Set rst=Server.CreateObject("ADODB.Command")
            SQL="SELECT * FROM mylib.myfile WHERE ITEMNO=' " & ITEM & "' "
        rst.Open SQL, conn
        %>
```

Each time the statement is executed, the query optimizer will analyze it. You insert the desired value into the SQL statement at execution time, through the use of concatenation.

The following example performs the same function, through the use of parameters:

```
        <%
            Set conn=Server.CreateObject("ADODB.Connection")
            conn.ConnectionString="Provider=IBMDA400; Data Source=S1234567; " &_
```

```
                        "User ID=user;Password=secret; "
        conn.open
        Set cmd=Server.CreateObject("ADODB.Command")
        cmd.CommandText="SELECT * FROM mylib.myfile WHERE ITEMNO=?"
        cmd.Parameters(0)=Item
        Set rst=cmd.Execute
    %>
```

While the functionality is the same as in the previous example, the query optimizer only needs to analyze the query when the CommandText property is set. When the value of the Item field needs to be changed, the Recordset object would be closed, the parameter value would be changed to the new value, and the Recordset would be reopened. This technique allows you to achieve some performance improvements when repeatedly reading from the same database.

For a list of properties, methods, and collections commonly used with the Command object, see Table 3.5.

Table 3.5: The Properties, Methods, and Collections of the ADO Command Object

Item	Type	Description
ActiveConnection	Property	Identifies the page containing the current record. The total record count is divided into pages as defined on the PageSize property.
CommandText	Property	Defines the text of the source for the Command object.
CommandTimeout	Property	Specifies the amount of time the command is allowed to run before a timeout occurs.
CommandType	Property	Defines the type of command to be issued.
Execute	Method	Runs the SQL statement or stored procedure defined on the CommandText property.
Parameters	Collection	Allows you to set the value of parameters within the CommandText property of the Command object.
Properties	Collection	Used to access specific attributes of the Command object.Command object.

ADO Error Object

The ADO Error object directly relates to the Errors collection of the Connection object. It allows you to retrieve information when an error occurs while attempting to use one of the ADO objects. The code shown in Figure 3.5 shows how the Error object would be used.

This example defines an ADO Connection and opens a Recordset object. Next, it uses the For Each..In statement to move each item within the Connection object's Errors collection into the ADO Error object named "errs." It then writes the Description property of the Error object to the browser, using the Response.Write method. This property contains descriptive text for any errors within the collection. When an error occurs using the IBMDA400 OLE DB provider, this property will contain the full error text generated on the iSeries. In most cases, this will be the same error description that would be written to the job log on the iSeries.

A Practical Example

To see just exactly how an application would use ADO with ASP, let's step through a simple Web application that displays field information for a given file. This application is comprised of two Active Server Pages. The first page allows the user to select the file for which he or she would like to see field information. The second page displays the actual field information for the selected file.

```
<%
    Set conn=Server.CreateObject("ADODB.Connection")
    conn.ConnectionString="Provider=IBMDA400; Data Source=S1234567; "&_
                    "User ID=user;Password=secret; "
    conn.open

    Set errs=Server.CreateObject("ADODB.Error")
    Set rst=Server.CreateObject("ADODB.Recordset")
    rst,Open "SELECT * FROM mylib.myfile", conn
    For Each errs IN conn.Errors
        Response.Write errs.Description
    Next
%>
```

Figure 3.5: This example displays ADO errors to the browser window using the Error object.

The first page of this example, named "Files.asp," is shown in Figure 3.6. It starts by creating the ADO connection in the same way as in previous examples. After creating the Connection object, it opens a Recordset object, which accesses the file systables in qsys2 library. This logical file is used to offer compatibility with other versions of SQL. It contains information for every file on your system.

```
<!-- #include file="adovbs.inc" -->
<html><head></head>
<body>
<form name=fileselect method=GET action="fields.asp">
<table>
<tr><td>File Name:</td><td><select name=file>
<%
    Set conn=Server.CreateObject("ADODB.Connection")
    conn.ConnectionString="Provider=IBMDA400; Data Source=S1234567; " &_
                    "User ID=user;Password=secret; "
    conn.open

    Set rst=Server.CreateObject("ADODB.Recordset")
    rst.Open "SELECT TABLE_NAME, TABLE_SCHEMA FROM QSYS2.SYSTABLES", _
            conn, adOpenKeyset

    rst.MoveFirst

    Do Until rst.EOF
    Response.Write "<option value=' " & rst.Fields(1) & _
        "/" & rst.Fields(0) & ">"
    Response.Write rst.Fields(1) & "/" & rst.Fields(0)& _
    "</option>"
    rst.MoveNext
    Loop
    End If
    rst.Close
    conn.Close
%>
</select></td></tr>
<tr><td rowspan=2>
<input type=SUBMIT value="Display Fields"></td></tr>
</table>
</form>
</body>
</html>
```

Figure 3.6: This page allows a user to select a file name from a drop-down list.

The SYSCOLUMNS file, which is used in the second page of the example, is also an SQL standard file. It contains field-level information for each of the files listed in systables. Each of the file and library names is retrieved from the Recordset object and used as a list-box item within an HTML form on a Web page. To be able to pass both the library and file names in one field to the second page of the application, the values are concatenated into the OS/400-standard "library/file" format.

After saving this file to your Web server as "Files.asp," you should be able to open the page by accessing the URL *http://servername/files.asp*, where *server-name* is the name or IP address of your Web server. Figure 3.7 shows what the output from this page will look like when displayed in a browser window.

The second page in the application takes the file name provided through the "file" Querystring variable and display a list of the fields in that file. Figure 3.8 contains the source for this Active Server Page, called "Fields.asp."

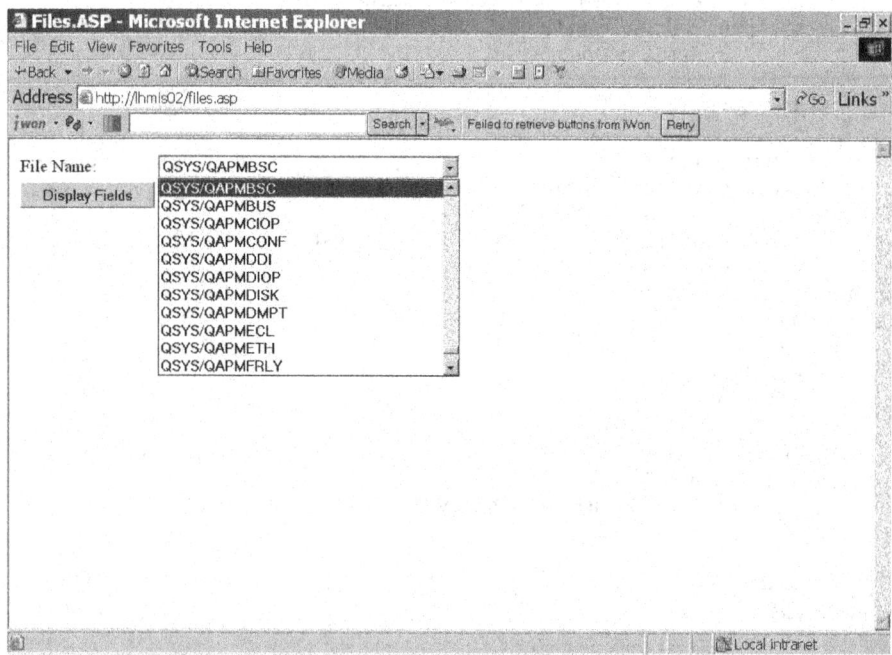

Figure 3.7: The page Files.asp is displayed in a Web browser.

```
<!-- #include file="adovbs.inc" -->
<html><head></head>
<body>
<table>
<%
   Set conn=Server.CreateObject("ADODB.Connection")
   conn.ConnectionString="DRIVER=Client Access ODBC Driver (32-bit); "&_
                         "UID=USER;PWD=SECRET;SYSTEM=192.168.0.5"

   conn.open
   FileLib= Request.Querystring("File")
   Slash= InStr(FileLib, "/")
   Lib=Left(FileLib,Slash-1)
   File=Right(FileLib, Len(FileLib)-Slash)

   Set cmd=Server.CreateObject("ADODB.Command")

   Sql="SELECT FIELD_NAME, DESC, LENGTH FROM QSYS2.SYSCOLUMNS WHERE "&_
       "TBNAME = ? AND TABLE_SCHEMA = ? "
   cmd.ActiveConnection=conn
   cmd.CommandText=Sql
   cmd.Parameters(0)=File
   cmd.Parameters(1)=Lib

   Set rst = Server.CreateObject("ADODB.Recordset")

   With rst
      .CursorType = adOpenStatic
      Set .Source = cmd
      .Open
End With

Response.Write "<tr>"
For X=0 to rst.Fields.Count-1
   Response.Write "<th>" & rst.Fields(X).Name & "</th>"
Next
Response.Write "</tr>"

Do Until rst.EOF
   Response.Write "<tr>"

   For X=0 to rst.Fields.Count-1
      Response.Write "<td>" " & rst.Fields(X).Value & "</td>"
   Next
      Response.Write "</tr>"
   rst.MoveNext
```

Figure 3.8: The second page of the ASP application displays field information (part 1 of 2).

```
Loop
End If
    rst.Close
    conn.Close
%>
</tr>
</table>
</body>
</html>
```

Figure 3.8: The second page of the ASP application displays field information (part 2 of 2).

This page uses the same technique to access the ADO objects as Files.asp. This time, however, the data read is being incorporated into an HTML table. Fields.asp starts out, as usual, by defining the Connection object. Next, it starts breaking the value passed through the FileLib Querystring variable into separate fields by determining the position of the slash character, using the InStr VBScript function. This value is used with the Left function to strip out the library name from the left side of the string. It then uses the Right function to get the file name from the right side of the string. These values supply the parameters of the Command object.

Next, the Recordset object is created. A With group defines the CursorType property, and then the Source property is set to the Command object. Finally, the Open method opens the Recordset. These steps must be used to define the cursor type for a Recordset that is based on a Command object.

The field names are retrieved from items within the Recordset's Fields collection, using the Name property. These values are displayed within the HTML table's heading using the <TH> and </TH> tags. Next, the code reads through each record of the Recordset and displays the field information as table data, using the <TD> and </TD> HTML tags. Finally, the Recordset and Connection objects are closed. Figure 3.9 shows the output from this page in a Web browser.

Adding Error-handling

Using the techniques just discussed, you can easily create custom reports that retrieve data from the iSeries—or from any other data source that is OLE DB or

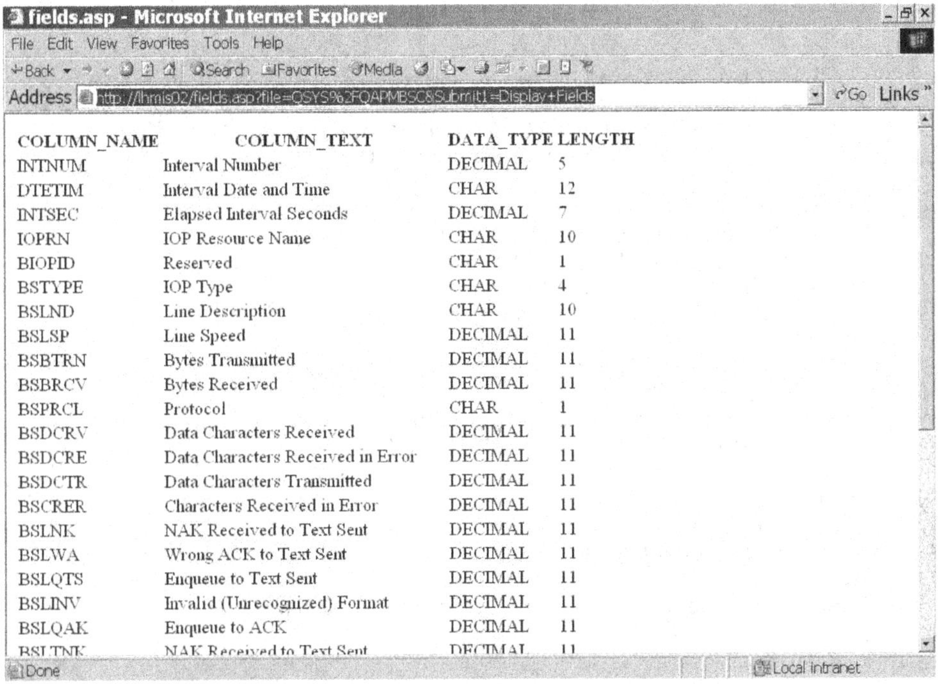

COLUMN_NAME	COLUMN_TEXT	DATA_TYPE	LENGTH
INTNUM	Interval Number	DECIMAL	5
DTETIM	Interval Date and Time	CHAR	12
INTSEC	Elapsed Interval Seconds	DECIMAL	7
IOPRN	IOP Resource Name	CHAR	10
BIOPID	Reserved	CHAR	1
BSTYPE	IOP Type	CHAR	4
BSLND	Line Description	CHAR	10
BSLSP	Line Speed	DECIMAL	11
BSBTRN	Bytes Transmitted	DECIMAL	11
BSBRCV	Bytes Received	DECIMAL	11
BSPRCL	Protocol	CHAR	1
BSDCRV	Data Characters Received	DECIMAL	11
BSDCRE	Data Characters Received in Error	DECIMAL	11
BSDCTR	Data Characters Transmitted	DECIMAL	11
BSCRER	Characters Received in Error	DECIMAL	11
BSLNK	NAK Received to Text Sent	DECIMAL	11
BSLWA	Wrong ACK to Text Sent	DECIMAL	11
BSLQTS	Enqueue to Text Sent	DECIMAL	11
BSLINV	Invalid (Unrecognized) Format	DECIMAL	11
BSLQAK	Enqueue to ACK	DECIMAL	11
BSLTNK	NAK Received to Text Sent	DECIMAL	11

Figure 3.9: Fields.asp is displayed in a Web browser.

ODBC compliant, for that matter. One thing that wasn't addressed in the previous example, however, is error-handling. If an error were to occur with any of the ADO objects, an error message would be displayed in the browser window. To get around this possibility, you can modify Fields.asp as shown in Figure 3.10.

In this version of Fields.asp, the "On Error Resume Next" statement disables all error-trapping of the ASP code. The added section of code first creates an ADO Error object, and then uses the For Each..In statement to assign each item within the Errors collection to the Error object "errs." All of the error-description values are concatenated into a single string. Next, the Response.Write statement inserts a client script into the document. This client script will display the error message in a Windows message box, using the MsgBox function. The Window.Navigate method redirects control to the first page of the application. This shows more of the power of ASP: not only can you create HTML dynamically at execution time, but you can even create client-side scripts from a server-side script.

```
<%
   On Error Resume Next
   Set conn=Server.CreateObject("ADODB.Connection")
   conn.ConnectionString="DRIVER=Client Access ODBC Driver (32-bit); "&_
                         "UID=USER;PWD=SECRET;SYSTEM=192.168.0.5"

   conn.open
   FileLib= Request.Querystring("File")
   Slash= InStr(FileLib, "/")
   Lib=Left(FileLib,Slash-1)
   File=Right(FileLib, Len(FileLib)-Slash)

   Set cmd=Server.CreateObject("ADODB.Command")

   Sql="SELECT FIELD_NAME, DESC, LENGTH FROM QSYS2.SYSCOLUMNS WHERE " &_
      " TBNAME = ? AND TABLE_SCHEMA = ? "
   cmd.ActiveConnection=conn
   cmd.CommandText=Sql
   cmd.Parameters(0)=File
   cmd.Parameters(1)=Lib

   Set rst = Server.CreateObject("ADODB.Recordset")

   With rst
      .CursorType = adOpenStatic
      Set .Source = cmd
      .Open
   End With

'Inserted Code Block
   Set err=Server.CreateObject("ADODB.Error")
   ErrorStr=""
   For Each err In conn.Errors
      ErrorStr=ErrorStr & err.Description
   Next
   If ErrorStr<>"" Then
      Response.Write "<Script Language='VBScript'>"
      Response.Write "MsgBox " & Chr(34) & ErrorStr & Chr(34)
      Response.Write "Window.Navigate " & Chr(34) & "file.asp" & _
      Chr(34)
      Response.Write "</Script>"
   End If
'Inserted Code Block

   rst.MoveFirst
   Response.Write "<tr>"
```

Figure 3.10: Error-handling code is added to Fields.asp (part 1 of 2).

```
    For X=0 to rst.Fields.Count-1
        Response.Write "<th>" & rst.Fields(X).Name & "</th>"
    Next
    Response.Write "</tr>"

    Do Until rst.EOF
        Response.Write "<tr>"

        For X=0 to rst.Fields.Count-1
            Response.Write "<td>" & rst.Fields(X).Value & "</td>"
        Next
        Response.Write "</tr>"
        rst.MoveNext
    Loop
    End If
    rst.Close
    conn.Close
%>
```

Figure 3.10: Error-handling code is added to Fields.asp (part 2 of 2).

Increasing Efficiency

You can also incorporate other ASP objects into this application to make it more efficient. For example, since both pages of the application use identical Connection objects, you can store the Connection object in a Session variable. This allows you to only make the connection once within the application, and leave the connection open throughout the time that a session is running. You would do this by replacing the following two lines in both Files.asp and Fields.asp:

```
    Set conn=Server.CreateObject("ADODB.Connection")
    conn.ConnectionString="DRIVER=Client Access ODBC Driver (32-bit); "&_
                    "UID=USER;PWD=SECRET;SYSTEM=192.168.0.5"

    conn.open
```

These lines would be replaced with the code shown here:

```
    If Session("conn") = "" Then
        Set conn=Server.CreateObject("ADODB.Connection")
```

```
conn.ConnectionString="DRIVER=Client Access ODBC Driver (32-bit);"&_
                      "UID=USER;PWD=SECRET;SYSTEM=192.168.0.5"

conn.open
Session("conn")=conn
Else
conn=Session("conn")
End If
```

This modified code first checks to see if the Session variable named "conn" exists. If this Session variable doesn't exist, the Connection object is created and saved into the Session variable. If it does exist, the Session object is moved into the "conn" object. One other modification would need to be made: the conn.Close method would have to be removed from both pages.

It's important to note that the Client Access OLE DB provider doesn't function well using a Connection object stored in a Session variable. For this reason, the ODBC driver shown is really the best option if you want to store your ADO Connection object in a Session variable. As a general rule, any ASP application that is comprised of a set of Active Server Pages used for a single Web application can share a common Connection object using this same technique. Doing this can return some performance improvements within your application.

Summary

The examples in this chapter illustrate the basic building blocks for creating data-access pages using ASP. The ability to access an external data source like the iSeries from an ASP is one of the most important components to creating ASP applications. In the coming chapters, you'll use these same techniques when building complete ASP applications.

4

Converting to ASP

The first three chapters of this book examine just what Active Server Pages are and how to get data from the iSeries into an ASP. This chapter shows you how to take existing applications on the iSeries and convert them to ASP applications. You'll examine how specific RPG operation codes would be performed in ASP using VBScript. You'll also see how application functions like subfile displays can be emulated in an Active Server Page. To make the transition go a little more smoothly, you'll explore some custom VBScript functions that emulate RPG operation codes.

RPG Operation Codes

One of the keys to converting an RPG application into ASP is learning how the tasks performed by RPG op codes are done in ASP VBScript. Believe it or not, it's actually possible to draw correlations between RPG op codes and functions in VBScript. Some of these correlations might be fairly obvious. For example, consider a function that would be performed on the EVAL op code:

```
C                 EVAL       X=12*Y                          RPG EVAL
```

In VBScript, this would simply be replaced with a calculation, as shown here:

```
X = 12 * Y                                              'VBScript
```

Another example of an RPG op code with a fairly obvious VBScript equivalent is an IF..ENDIF group.

Some specific RPG op codes and their VBScript alternatives are discussed in the following pages. This is not a complete list of all RPG op codes. Some op codes have been specifically excluded because there are no VBScript equivalents. In most cases, these op codes are related to RPG-specific operations that are not required in VBScript. These cases will probably require that you reconsider the overall design of your application.

ADD

The ADD op code is used as shown below to add a value to the field specified in the result field:

```
C                        ADD      12       FLDA
```

In VBScript, this would be replaced by the following simple mathematical calculation:

```
FLDA = FLDA + 12
```

This would also be true for the other mathematical operators (such as DIV, MULT, and SUB).

BEGSR..ENDSR

The BEGSR and ENDSR op codes define the beginning and end of an RPG subroutine, as shown below:

```
C          SUBR1      BEGSR
*
C                     ENDSR
```

This would be replaced by either a VBScript subroutine or function, as shown here:

```
Function Subr1()
'
End Function
```

CALL

The RPG CALL op code is used to run an external program. It is coded as shown below:

```
C                   CALL      'PGM001'
C                   PARM                        PARAM1
```

In VBScript, you have a few options. You could replace the external program with a VBScript function, like this:

```
CALL PGM001(PARAM1)
```

Alternatively, if the external program performs a task that is not interactive, the CALL can be replaced by an ADO Command object, as shown here:

```
Set cmd=Server.CreateObject("ADODB.Command")
cmd.CommandText= "{call pgm001 parm(?)}"
cmd.ActiveConnection=conn
cmd.Parameters(0)=Param1
cmd.Execute
```

This solution would be ideally suited to call an application that simply returns a value to the caller.

COMP

The COMP op code controls the state of an RPG indicator based on the comparison of two values, as shown here:

```
C          FIELD1      COMP      FIELD2                      95
```

While this type of operation can simply be replaced by an If statement, you can also use the VBScript shown below to emulate a COMP statement:

```
IN95 = (FIELD1=FIELD2)
```

This statement will return a Boolean value (either True or False) based on the condition shown in parentheses. In this example, the value of IN95 will be True if Field1 equals Field2. Otherwise, it will be False.

DO

The RPG DO..ENDDO loop performs a set of tasks for a defined number of times, as shown in the sample code below:

```
C          1           DO        25                          VAR1
*
C                      ENDDO
```

In an ASP VBScript, this would be replaced by a For..Next loop, as shown here:

```
FOR VAR1 = 1 TO 25
  *
NEXT
```

DOWxx, DOUxx

The DOUxx and DOWxx op codes perform a set of RPG statements as long as a defined condition exists, as shown below:

```
C            CHK         DOWEQ      *OFF
  *
C                        ENDDO
```

These op codes have VBScript equivalents in the form of the Do..Until and Do..While statements. A Do..While example is shown here:

```
DO WHILE CHK=FALSE
 '
LOOP
```

EXFMT

The EXFMT op code sends the specified display-file record format to the screen, as shown below:

```
C                        EXFMT      FORMAT1
```

Since an Active Server Page doesn't use a display file, there's really no exact correlation for this. The closest equivalent would be to use the Response.Flush command to send the contents of the Response buffer to the browser, like this:

```
        Response.Flush
```

It's important to remember, however, that this will only send the ASP output to the browser. Unlike the EXFMT op code, your ASP code will not accept input back from the browser prior to continuing execution. You'll see how to deal with this a little later in this chapter.

EXSR

The EXSR op code transfers control to an RPG subroutine, as shown here:

```
        C                           EXSR        SUBR1
```

As explained earlier, the RPG subroutine would be replaced by a VBScript function. This function would then be executed as shown here:

```
        CALL SUBR1()
```

GOTO

The GOTO op code transfers to the TAG statement specified on factor 2, as shown here:

```
        C                           GOTO        RED01
```

While the Visual Basic programming language itself supports the Goto statement, VBScript does not. Therefore, it is not available in an Active Server Page.

IF/IFxx..ELSE..ENDIF

The IF and IFxx statements conditionally perform a set of RPG statements based on a defined condition, as shown below:

```
C                       IF      X>0
   * If the result is true
C                       ELSE
   * If the result is false
C                       ENDIF
```

VBScript offers an If statement that is used in a very similar manner. Here is an example:

```
If X>0 Then
' If the result is true
Else
' If the result is false
End If
```

OPEN

The OPEN op code opens a file that has been defined as user-controlled for opening and closing, as shown here:

```
C                       OPEN    FILE
```

Assuming that the file to be opened is a data file, this would be replaced with a Recordset.Open statement to open an ADO Recordset, as explained in chapter 3.

READ (READP, READE, REDPE)

The READ op codes retrieve the next or previous record from the specified file, as shown here:

```
C                       READ    FILE
*
C                       READP   FILEA
```

When using an ADO Recordset, this op code would be replaced by the Recordset.MoveNext or Recordset.MovePrev op code:

```
File.MoveNext
        *
FileA.MovePrev
```

The READE and REDPE op codes read the next value with a key field matching the value specified in factor 1. You have two options for handling this. First, you could define the Recordset using "WHERE" and "ORDER BY" SQL clauses to select and sort the records, and then simply use the MoveNext and MovePrev methods to navigate the Recordset. Second, you could use the ADO Seek method.

The RPG code shown here would read the next record with a matching key field:

```
C            KEY        READE     FILE1
```

Using the first method, this would be handled with the Command object, as shown below:

```
Set cmd=Server.CreateObject("ADODB.Command")

Sql="SELECT * FROM FILE1 WHERE " & _
    " KYFLD1 = ? ORDER BY KYFLD1, KYFLD2 "
cmd.ActiveConnection=conn
cmd.CommandText=Sql
cmd.Parameters(0)=KEY

Set rst = Server.CreateObject("ADODB.Recordset")

With rst
   .CursorType = adOpenKeyset
   Set .Source = cmd
   .Open
End With
```

```
rst.MoveFirst
Response.Write rst.Fields(0)
rst.MoveNext
```

This example creates the Recordset object based on a Command object to allow you to define a parameter or parameters to act as key fields. To redefine the key fields, you close the Recordset, change the parameter values, and then reopen the Recordset.

Using the Seek method avoids repeatedly opening the Recordset object because you can find a certain record based on defined key-field values. It's important to note that an SQL statement cannot be supplied as the source for a Recordset that uses the Seek method. Instead, a file and library name must be supplied in the format "library/file," as shown here:

```
Set rst = Server.CreateObject("ADODB.Recordset")
rst.index="PrimaryKey"
rst.Open "lib/file1", adOpenKeyset
Set KeyList=Array(KYFLD1,KEYFLD2)
rst.Seek  KeyList, adSeekFirst
```

The search values for the two key fields are inserted into an array in the order in which they appear in the file. This is similar to the way a KLIST is used in an RPG program.

RETRN (RETURN)

The RETRN op code returns control to the program that called the current program. In VBScript, subroutines support this same function, using the Return statement.

SCAN

The SCAN op code searches a supplied string field for a specified string value. If a match is found, the starting position of the match is returned to the specified result field. This is shown in the example below:

```
C                STRINGA    SCAN      'ABC':2        POSTN
```

In this example, the field STRINGA will be searched for the literal "ABC" starting in position 2. If a match is made, the starting position within STRINGA of the match will be moved into the field POSTN.

This same function would be accomplished in VBScript using the InStr ("in string") function, as shown here:

```
Postn=InStr(2,Stringa, "ABC")
```

In this example, the first parameter represents the position within the string where the search should begin. The string to be searched is supplied as the second parameter, and the search value is provided in the third parameter.

SELEC (SELECT)..WHxx..ENDSL

The SELEC op code conditionally performs portions of code based on the value of a specified field, as shown here:

```
C                              SELECT
C                              WHEN      X=1
* code for when X is 1
C                              WHEN      X=2
* code for when X is 2
C                              OTHER
* code for all other possibilities
C                              ENDSL
```

VBScript supports a similar version of this function in its Select Case statement, which is shown in the following example:

```
Select Case X
   Case 1
      ' code for when X is 1
   Case 2
      ' code for when X is 2
   Case Else
      ' code for all other possibilities
End Select
```

This code would perform the same function as the SELEC RPG op code, with slightly different syntax.

SETGT/SETLL

The SETGT and SETLL op codes position a file cursor directly before or after the key value specified in factor 1, as shown below:

```
C           KEY         SETLL       FILE1
```

This would be replaced using the same technique described earlier for READE or REDPE. You'll examine this, as well as other data-file access concepts, a little later in this chapter.

SETON/SETOF

The SETON and SETOF op codes turn an RPG indicator on or off. While VBScript doesn't support indicators per se, it does support Boolean fields, which can be used to store an "On/Off" value in much the same way an RPG indicator does.

SORTA

The SORTA op code sorts the contents of an array based on the sequence (ascending or descending) defined on the extension or definition specs for the array. An example of the SORTA op code is shown here:

```
C                              SORTA      ARRAY1
```

VBScript doesn't have a function to sort an array. However, a user-defined function could easily be created for this purpose. The code for this function is shown in Figure 4.1.

```
Function SortStrArray(Array, Ord)
If Ord="" Then Ord="ASC"
    For X=0 to ubound(Array)
        For Y=X+1 to ubound(Array)
            If X<>Y And Array(X)<>"" AND Array(Y)<>"" Then
                If (Ord="ASC" and Array(X) > Array(Y)) OR _
                   (Ord="DESC" and Array(X) < Array(Y)) Then
                   Temp=Array(Y)
                   Array(Y)=Array(X)
                   Array(Y)=Temp
                End If
            End If
        Next
    Next
Set SortStrArray=Array
End Function
```

Figure 4.1: This VBScript function will sort array elements.

This function has two parameters: the array to be sorted, and the order in which to sort the array. The function reads through the array to place all of the items in the proper order.

SUBST

The SUBST op code extracts a portion of one string into another. Here's an example of how this op code is used:

```
C         2         SUBST      STRINGA:5             STRINGB
```

This example would move the characters from STRINGA, starting at the second character and going five characters over, into the field STRINGB. This would be accomplished in VBScript using the Mid function, as shown here:

```
Stringb=Mid(STRINGA,2,5)
```

When using the Mid function, the first parameter defines the source string. The second parameter defines the starting position, and the third parameter identifies the number of characters to go over from the starting position.

TESTN

The TESTN op code tests if a field is numeric or contains blanks. The following example would test the field FLDA and turn on indicator 55 if it contained all numeric values, or 56 if it were blank:

```
C              TESTN          FLDA          55  56
```

IsNumeric is the VBScript alternative to this op code. The field to be tested is supplied as the only parameter to this function. The IsNumeric function will return a Boolean value when used as shown here:

```
IN55=IsNumeric(FLDA)
```

TIME

The RPG TIME op code moves the current time to the specified field, as shown in the following example:

```
C              TIME           TIMFLD      6 0
```

This example populates the field named TIMFLD with the current time. In VBScript, this would be performed using the Now() function, as shown here:

```
TIMFLD=NOW()
```

UPDAT (UPDATE)

The UPDAT op code writes out any changes to the current record in the record format defined on factor 2, as shown in the following example:

```
C                    UPDATE    REC001
```

The best alternative in VBScript is to create an SQL statement to update the desired record based on specified key field values. The following example uses the "RRN()" SQL function to determine the relative record number of a given record, and then uses that value to update the specified record:

```
Set rst = Server.CreateObject("ADODB.Recordset")
rst.Open "SELECT ITEM, LOCN, ONHAND, RRN() AS RECN FROM " & _
        "ITEMMSTR WHERE ITEM='ABC123'", adOpenKeyset
rst.MoveFirst

NewBal=rst.Fields("ONHAND") - ADJQTY
RecordNum=rst.Fields("RECN")
rst.Close

Set cmd=Server.CreateObject("ADODB.Command")

Sql="UPDATE ITEMMSTR SET OHNAHD=? WHERE " & _
    " RRN() = ? "
cmd.ActiveConnection=conn
cmd.CommandText=Sql
cmd.Parameters(0)=NewBal
cmd.Parameters(1)=RecordNum

cmd.Execute
```

This example captures the current record number for the current record by reading the value of RRN(). It then updates the balance using the RRN() function as the criteria.

WRITE

The WRITE op code writes out a new record to the file-record format specified in factor 2, as shown here:

```
C                         WRITE     REC001
```

The VBScript alternative to this involves using an ADO Command object that's based on an SQL "INSERT" statement, as shown below:

```
Set cmd=Server.CreateObject("ADODB.Command")

Sql="INSERT INTO REC001 VALUES(? ? ? ?) "
cmd.ActiveConnection=conn
cmd.CommandText=Sql
cmd.Parameters(0)=ITEM
cmd.Parameters(1)=CUST
cmd.Parameters(2)=QTY
cmd.Parameters(3)=PRICE
cmd.Execute
```

This example uses a similar process to that used to replace the UPDAT op code.

XFOOT

The XFOOT op code sums all of the elements from an array into the field specified as the result. Here is an example:

```
C                         XFOOT     ARR              TOTAL
```

This example would summarize the values from the array named ARR into the field TOTAL.

There is no simple function to replace this. The VBScript alternative would be to use a For..Next loop, as shown here:

```
Total=0
For X=0 to ubound(arr)
   Total=Total+Arr(X)
Next X
```

This VBScript first sets the value of the field Total to zero. Then, a For..Next loop reads through each of the array elements and adds it to Total. The Ubound() VBScript function identifies the maximum number of values in an array.

Program Conversion

Now that you've seen some parallels between RPG op codes and VBScript functions, let's take a broader look at converting an interactive application into ASP. We'll start by examining a simple application that uses many of the techniques commonly used in RPG applications, including file read and write operations and subfile displays.

While understanding the similarities between RPG op codes and VBScript functions is important, it's not likely that you will want to convert an RPG application line-for-line into an ASP application. It's more probable that you'll want to take the overall program flow used within the RPG application and transfer that logic into VBScript in your ASP.

Display-file Source

As you've already discovered, the equivalent of the display file in an ASP application is the HTML source created dynamically by the ASP. Figure 4.2 contains the DDS display-file source named SAMP01FM, which is used by the sample application.

This source contains four record formats. FORMAT01 contains a single input/ output field that is used to enter a search-item number. The display-file record format FORMAT02 acts as the header for FORMAT03, which is a subfile record used to display a list of items. Finally, FORMAT04 is the subfile control record for FORMAT03 and is also used to modify item details. Since ASP applications contain the code and display information in one source, you need to take a look at

```
A*================================================================
A* To compile:
A*
A*        CRTDSPF    FILE(LIB/SAMP01FM) SRCFILE(LIB/QDDSSRC)
A*
A*================================================================
A                                            DSPSIZ(24 80 *DS3)
A                                            PRINT
A                                            CA03
A            R FORMAT01
A                                            TEXT('Command keys')
A                                      22  4'F3=Exit'
A                                            COLOR(BLU)
A                                       1 29'Item Maintenance'
A                                            DSPATR(HI)
A                                       5  3'Item Search:'
A              SRITEM         15A  B    5 16
A            R FORMAT02
A                                            TEXT('Command keys')
A                                       4  1'Sel Item  Description -
A                                            Weight        -
A                                            '
A                                            DSPATR(HI)
A                                            DSPATR(UL)
A                                       1 31'Item Listing'
A                                            DSPATR(HI)
A            R FORMAT03                       SFL
A              SEL             1   B    5  3
A 66                                          DSPATR(PR)
A              SFITEM         15   O    5  6
A              SFDESC         35   O    5 22
A              SFWGHT         15  5O    5 58EDTWRD('       .      ')
A            R FORMAT04                       SFLCTL(FORMAT03)
A                                            CA12
A                                            OVERLAY
A 35                                          SFLDSP
A 35                                          SFLDSPCTL
A 36                                          SFLCLR
A 35                                          SFLEND(*MORE)
A                                            SFLSIZ(9999)
A                                            SFLPAG(0013)
A              RRN             4S OH          SFLRCDNBR
A                                      21  1'Item:'
A              ITEM           15   B   21  7
A 78                                          DSPATR(PR)
A 76                                          ERRMSG('ERROR-Item Exists' 66)
```

Figure 4.2: This display file is used within the sample application (part 1 of 2).

```
A                DESC          35  B   21 29
A                                      21 23'Desc'
A                                      22  1'Weight:'
A                WEIGHT        15  5B  22  9EDTWRD('            .          ')
A                                      22 26'Length:'
A                LENGTH        15  5B  22 34EDTWRD('            .          ')
A                                      22 51'Width:'
A                WIDTH         15  5B  22 58EDTWRD('            .          ')
A                                      23  1'Retail:'
A                RETAIL        15  5B  23  9EDTWRD('            .          ')
A                                      23 26'St Cs'
A                STDCST        15  5B  23 34EDTWRD('            .          ')
A                                      24  4'F3=Exit          F12=CANCEL'
```

Figure 4.2: This display file is used within the sample application (part 2 of 2).

the RPG code associated with this application before you can consider conversion options.

ILE RPG Source

The RPG portion of this example performs both file access and display-file control. The ILE RPG code for SAMP01RG is shown in Figure 4.3.

This program uses a single physical file named ITEMMAS. The DDS source for this file can be found with the companion code for this book. The RPG code first outputs the display-file record format FORMAT01. The item number entered into this screen is used to determine the starting position for reading records into the subfile display. Figure 4.4 shows what the first screen of this example looks like.

The subfile records are written out for all items equal to or greater than the item entered. Prior to displaying the subfile display (formats FORMAT03 and FORMAT04), the header text for the subfile is written out by doing a WRITE to FORMAT02.

Once the subfile display is built and displayed, the application allows the user to select a record from the display and update the item in the lower portion of the screen. After the item is updated and the Enter key is pressed, the matching record is updated in the physical file. Figure 4.5 shows what the subfile display of the sample application looks like.

```
*================================================================
* To compile:
*
*       CRTBNDRPG  PGM(LIB/SAMP01RG) SRCFILE(LIB/QRPGLESRC)
*
*================================================================
FSAMP01FM  cf   e                 Workstn sfile(FORMAT03:rrn)

FITEMMAS   UF A E                 K Disk

D RRN              s              4 0

* Write out initial screen
C     First        Tag
C                  Exfmt     FORMAT01
C                  If        *INKC=*Off
* Build the subfile display
C     ReLoad       Tag
C                  Eval      RRN=0
C                  Eval      *IN36=*On
C                  Eval      *IN35=*Off
C                  Write     FORMAT04
C     SRITEM       SETLL     ITEMMAS
C                  READ      ITEMMAS
C                  DoW       Not %EOF(ITEMMAS)
C                  Eval      SFITEM=ITEMNO
C                  Eval      SFDESC=ITDESC
C                  Eval      SFWGHT=ITWGHT
C                  Eval      RRN=RRN+1
C                  Write     FORMAT03
C                  READ      ITEMMAS
C                  EndDo
C                  Eval      *IN66=*Off
C                  If        RRN=0
C                  Eval      SFDESC='No Items Found'
C                  Eval      *IN66=*On
C                  Eval      RRN=1
C                  Write     FORMAT03
C                  EndIf
C                  Eval      *IN36=*Off
C                  Eval      *IN35=*On
C                  Eval      *IN78=*Off
* Display subfile
C     ReDisp       Tag
C                  Eval      *IN36=*Off
C                  Eval      *IN35=*On
```

Figure 4.3: This simple application uses common RPG programming techniques (part 1 of 3).

```
     C                          Write      FORMAT02
     C                          Exfmt      FORMAT04
     C                          If         *INKC
     C                          Eval       *INLR=*ON
     C                          Return
     C                          EndIf
     C                          If         *INKL
     C                          Goto       First
     C                          EndIf
     * Update or Add Item Data
     C                          If         Item<>''
     C        ITEM              Chain      ITEMMAS
     C                          If         %Found(ITEMMAS)
     C                          If         *IN78
     C                          Eval       ITDESC=DESC
     C                          Eval       ITWGHT=WEIGHT
     C                          Eval       ITLNTH=LENGTH
     C                          Eval       ITWDTH=WIDTH
     C                          Eval       ITPRIC=RETAIL
     C                          Eval       ITCOST=STDCST
     C                          Update     ITEMMST
     C                          Clear                          FORMAT04
     C                          Eval       *IN78=*Off
     C                          Goto       ReLoad
     C                          Else
     C                          Eval       *IN76=*On
     C                          Goto       ReDisp
     C                          EndIf
     C                          EndIf
     C                          Clear                          ITEMMST
     C                          Eval       ITEMNO=ITEM
     C                          Eval       ITDESC=DESC
     C                          Eval       ITWGHT=WEIGHT
     C                          Eval       ITLNTH=LENGTH
     C                          Eval       ITWDTH=WIDTH
     C                          Eval       ITPRIC=RETAIL
     C                          Eval       ITCOST=STDCST
     C                          Clear                          FORMAT04
     C                          Write      ITEMMST
     C                          Else
     C                          ReadC      FORMAT03
     C                          If         %EOF(SAMP01FM)=*Off
     C        SFITEM            Chain      ITEMMAS
     C                          If         %Found(ITEMMAS)
     C                          Eval       ITEM=ITEMNO
     C                          Eval       DESC=ITDESC
```

Figure 4.3: This simple application uses common RPG programming techniques (part 2 of 3).

```
C                       Eval      WEIGHT=ITWGHT
C                       Eval      LENGTH=ITLNTH
C                       Eval      WIDTH=ITWDTH
C                       Eval      RETAIL=ITPRIC
C                       Eval      STDCST=ITCOST
C                       Eval      *IN78=*On
C                       EndIf
C                       EndIf
C                       EndIf
C                       EndIf
C                       Goto      ReDisp
   ***********************************************************************
```

Figure 4.3: This simple application uses common RPG programming techniques (part 3 of 3).

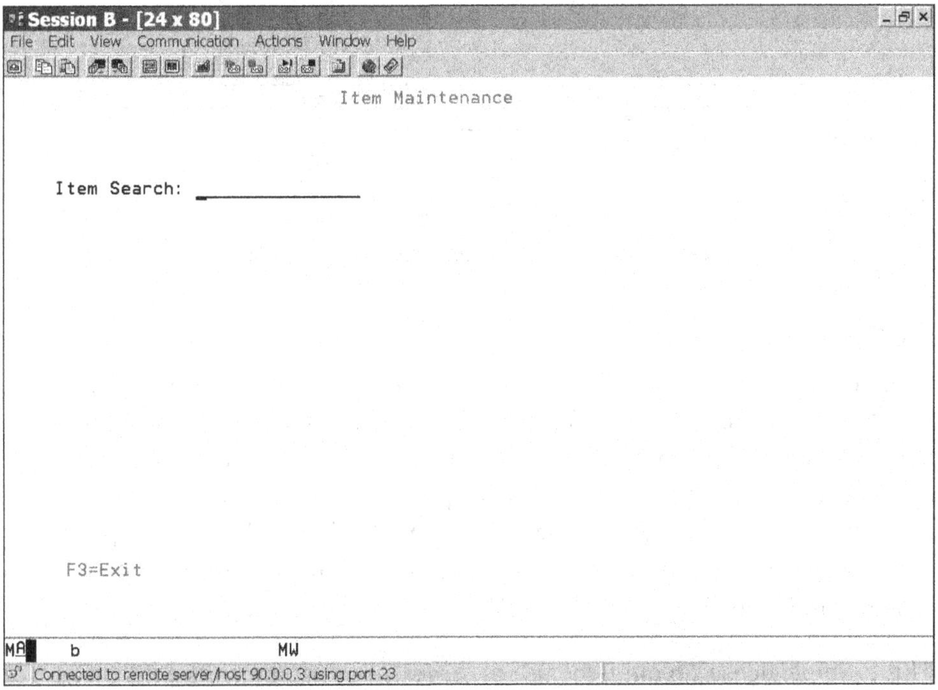

Figure 4.4: This screen is used to enter a search-item number.

This is a fairly basic example, but it performs a series of events that would be common to many of the applications that are probably running on your iSeries right now.

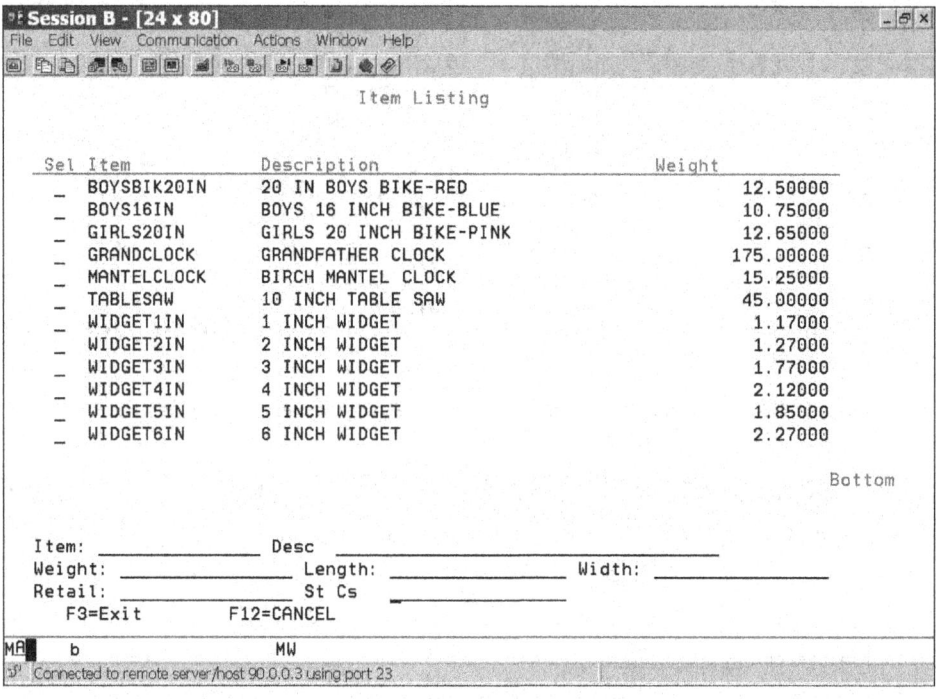

Figure 4.5: Items can be updated from this subfile display.

Conversion to ASP

When converting an application like this to ASP, you not only have to deal with how to achieve the file-access functionality, you also have to deal with things that affect the overall application flow, like subfiles and command keys. To start, let's create the modified version of the display file FORMAT01 as an HTML file called "Iteminput.html." Remember that the ASP will actually take the place of both the display file and the RPG program. The HTML code for Iteminput.html is shown in Figure 4.6.

This example doesn't require the use of server-side scripting, since it's just a simple HTML form to allow the user to enter the item. The output from this page is shown in Figure 4.7.

To replace the subfile display, you'll use a Web page that contains an HTML table to replicate the subfile records. This is done using the Active Server Page

```
<html>
<title>Item Search</title>
<body>
<form name=FORMAT01 action='itemlist.asp'>
    Item Search... <input type=TEXT name=SRITEM><br><br>
    <input type=SUBMIT value='List Items'>
</form>
</body>
</html>
```

Figure 4.6: This HTML is used to prompt the user for the item number.

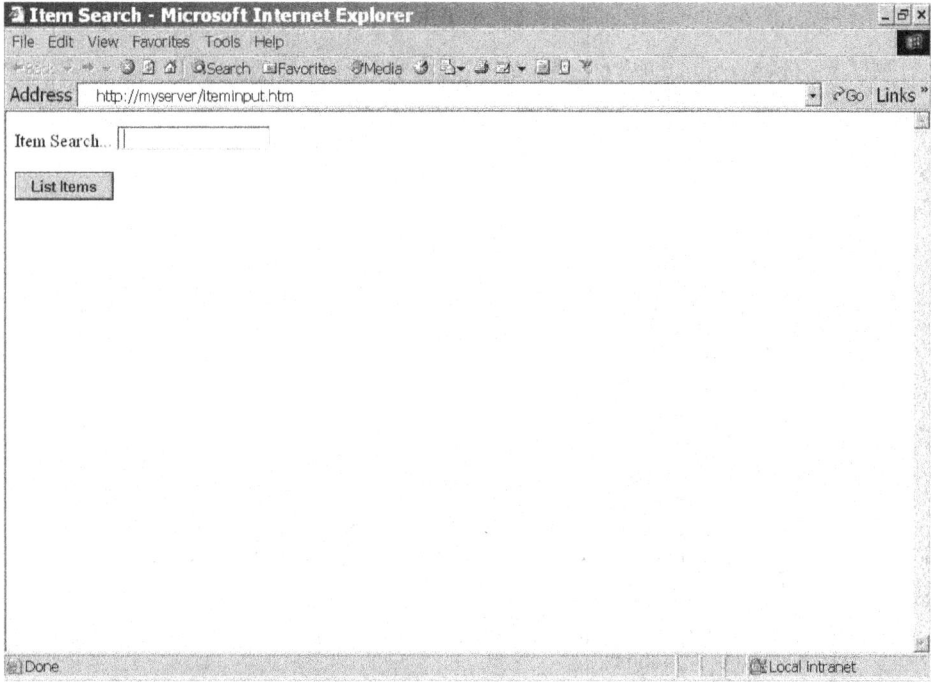

Figure 4.7: This is how Iteminput.html looks when displayed in a Web browser.

named "Items.asp." The portion of this page that creates the table is shown in Figure 4.8

```
<% set conn = Server.CreateObject("ADODB.Connection")
   conn.open "DRIVER=Client Access ODBC Driver (32-bit); " & _
             "UID=user; PWD=secret; System=192.168.0.1;"

   on error resume next
   ' Define number of lines per page
   lnperPg = 10
   ' set up a query to get the count, and another to get the data
   countSQL = "SELECT count(ITEMNO) FROM MYLIB.ITEMMAS
               WHERE ITEMNO>='" & _
               Request.Form("SRITEM") & "'"
   dataSQL = "SELECT * FROM ITEMMAS WHERE ITEMNO>='" & _
               Request.Form("SRITEM") & "' ORDER BY ITEMNO "

   ' Determine the number of records using the countSQL statement
   set rs=Server.CreateObject("ADODB.Recordset")

   rs.Open countSQL,conn,adOpenKeyset
   cnt = clng(rs(0))
   rs.close

   ' If no records, display message to the browser.
   if cnt < 1 then
      Response.Write "No records found."
      Response.End
   else
      if cnt = 1 then lnperpg = 1
      pages = clng(cnt/lnperpg)
      if cnt/lnperpg > pages then
         pages = pages + 1
      end if

      ' what page are we on?
      page = clng(request.form("page"))
      if Request.Form("command")="Next" then page=page+1
      if Request.Form("command")="Previous" then page=page-1
      if page <= 1 then
         page = 1
      elseif page > pages then
         page = pages
      end if
      cp = page
      Response.Write "<b>Item Listing</b> ... "
      Response.Write "<p><table border=0 cellpadding=4 "
      Response.Write "cellspacing=0 style='border:1px solid #999999'>"
   end if
```

Figure 4.8: This Active Server Page replaces the subfile in the RPG application (part 1 of 3).

```
' move to first record for the current screen
if pages > 1 then
   startrecord = (clng(page-1) * lnperpg) + 1
end if
' Open database        rs.Open dataSQL,conn,adOpenKeyset
rs.move(startrecord-1)


'display the fields names
Response.Write "<tr valign=middle>"
for y=0 to rs.fields.count-1
   Response.Write "<th>" & rs.fields(y).name & "</td>"
next
Response.Write "</tr>"


' Read from the database the number of records for a page or
' until EOF ' display values within the table
for x = 1 to lnperpg
   if not rs.eof then
   Response.Write "<tr valign=middle><td>
   <a href='itemupdate.asp?" & rs.fields(0).Name & "=" & _
   rs.Fields(0).Value
   for y=1 to rs.fields.count-1
      Response.Write "&" & rs.fields(y).Name & "=" & _
      rs.Fields(y).Value
   next
   Response.Write "' target='_blank'>" & _
   rs.Fields(0).Value & "</a></td>"
   for y=1 to rs.fields.count-1
      Response.Write "<td>" & rs.fields(y) & "</td>"
   next
   rs.movenext
   end if
next
Response.Write "</tr><tr>"
Response.Write "<form method='POST' name='FORMAT04'
   action='items.asp'>"
Response.Write "<td><input type=button name=CANCEL
   value='Cancel' " & _
   "onclick=" & chr(34) & "window.navigate('iteminput.htm');" & _
   chr(34) & "><input type=hidden  name=page value=" & page & _
   "><input name=SRITEM value='" & Request.Form("SRITEM") & _
   "' type='HIDDEN'></td><td></td><td></td><td></td><td></td><td>"
if page>1 then response.Write "<input type=submit name=command "& _
"value='Previous'>"
Response.Write "</td><td>"
```

Figure 4.8: This Active Server Page replaces the subfile in the RPG application (part 2 of 3).

```
        if pages>page then response.Write "<input type=submit
          name=command " & "value='Next'>"
        Response.Write "</td></form></tr></table>"
        ' close the Recordset and connection
        rs.close: set rs = nothing
        conn.close: set conn = nothing
    %>
```

Figure 4.8: This Active Server Page replaces the subfile in the RPG application (part 3 of 3).

This page takes the value provided through the Querystring variable SrItem and inserts this value into the "WHERE" clause of the Recordset's "SELECT" statement. This Recordset reads all records with an item number greater than or equal to the value of SrItem. The records are read, and the item information is listed within an HTML table.

This displays 10 items per page. If there are more records than will fit on one page, HTML form buttons are added to the bottom of the page to allow the user to move to the next or previous page. The ACTION attribute of the <FORM> tag refers back to this page. When the page is resubmitted, the value of the Command variable from the <INPUT> tag determines whether the Next or Previous button was clicked. This value also determine whether to increase or decrease the value of the form variable Page, which identifies the current page number. When this value is passed back into the page, the form fields that are used to update the item information are displayed at the top of the page, as shown in Figure 4.9.

Each item in the table contains a hyperlink that will open a new window containing Itemupdate.asp, which is a form for updating the item. The code for this page is shown in Figure 4.10.

This page creates an HTML form containing the values for the item selected on the previous screen. Each of the field values is fed into the screen through the Querystring. Notice that this example inserts values into the static HTML rather than writing the HTML using Response.Write. This alternative method can be useful in situations that require little VBScript processing and only need to read

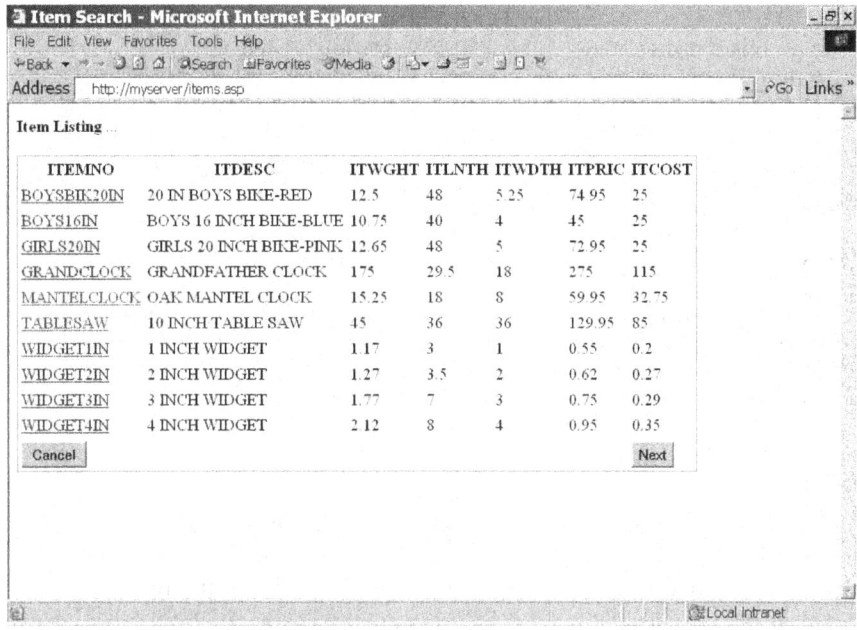

Figure 4.9: This page emulates a subfile using an HTML table.

```
<html>
<title>Item Update</title>
<body>
<form action="update.asp" method="post" name="UPDATE">
<table cellpadding=0 cellspacing=0 border=0>
<tr><td>Item:</td>
<td colspan=2><input type="TEXT" style="width:200" name=ITEMNO
value="<%=Request.querystring("ITEMNO")%>"></td>
<td>Description:</td>
<td colspan=2><input type="TEXT" style="width:300" name=ITDESC
value="<%=Request.querystring("ITDESC")%>"></td></tr>
<tr><td>Weight:</td>
<td><input type="TEXT" name=ITWGHT style="width:80;
text-align:right" value="<%=Request.querystring("ITWGHT")%>"></td>
<td>Length:</td>
<td><input type="TEXT" name=ITLNTH style="width:80;
text-align:right" value="<%=Request.querystring("ITLNTH")%>"></td>
<td>Width:</td>
```

Figure 4.10: This page acts as the "update" window for the application (part 1 of 2).

111

```
<td><input type="TEXT" name=ITWDTH style="width:80;
text-align:right" value="<%=Request.querystring("ITWDTH")%>">
</td></tr>
<tr><td>Price:</td>
<td><input type="TEXT" name=ITPRIC style="width:80;
text-align:right" value="<%=Request.querystring("ITPRIC")%>"></td>
<td></td><td></td><td>Std Cost:</td>
<td><input type="TEXT" name=ITCOST style="width:80;
text-align:right" value="<%=Request.querystring("ITCOST")%>">
</td></tr>
<tr><td colspan=6 align=center><input type="submit" name="update"
value="UPDATE"></td>
</tr></table>
</form>
</body>
</html>
```

Figure 4.10: This page acts as the "update" window for the application (part 2 of 2).

a value from a Querystring or form variable and write it to the browser. An example of the output of this page is shown in Figure 4.11.

The Update button on the form in Figure 4.11 will cause the modified item information to be written to the file. Updates can be cancelled by simply closing this window or using the browser's Back button. The ACTION property for this page's <FORM> tag is Update.asp. The code for this Active Server Page, shown in Figure 4.12, performs the file updates.

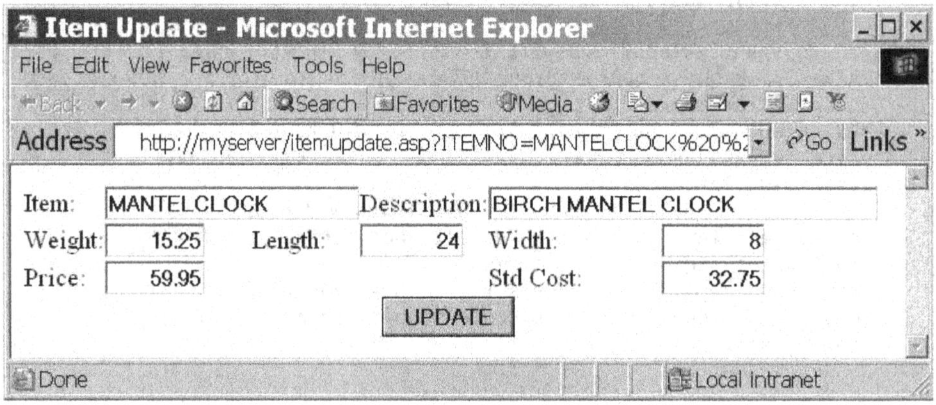

Figure 4.11: This page is used to update item information.

```
<html>
<title>Update</title>
<!-- #include file="adovbs.inc" -->
<BODY onload="window.close();" ONUNLOAD="opener.history.go(0);">
<%
   ' Define our connection object
   set conn = Server.CreateObject("ADODB.Connection")
   conn.open "DRIVER=Client Access ODBC Driver (32-bit); " & _
            "UID=user; PWD=secret; System=192.168.0.2;"

   'on error resume next

   set cmd=Server.CreateObject("ADODB.Command")
   cmd.ActiveConnection=conn
   cmd.CommandText = "UPDATE MYLIB.ITEMMAS SET ITDESC=?, ITWGHT=?," & -
      "ITLNTH=?, ITWDTH=?, ITPRIC=?, ITCOST=? WHERE ITEMNO=?"

   cmd.Parameters(0)=Left(TRIM(Request.Form("ITDESC")),35)
   cmd.Parameters(1)=Request.Form("ITWGHT")
   cmd.Parameters(2)=Request.Form("ITLNTH")
   cmd.Parameters(3)=Request.Form("ITWDTH")
   cmd.Parameters(4)=Request.Form("ITPRIC")
   cmd.Parameters(5)=Request.Form("ITCOST")
   cmd.Parameters(6)=Request.Form("ITEMNO")
   cmd.Execute
   Response.Write "Update Complete!"
   conn.close: set conn = nothing
%>
</body>
</html>
```

Figure 4.12: This Active Server Page performs file updates.

Notice that the page in Figure 4.12 doesn't display anything to the browser, since it just processes the request from the previous page to update the file. The ADO Command object updates the item information based on the item number selected. The ONLOAD event in the <BODY> HTML tag causes this window to close after the updates are complete. The ONUNLOAD event reloads the parent window when the "update" popup window closes. Update.asp remains invisible to the user because it never sends any output to the browser.

This example took you through the process of porting an interactive-subfile RPG application to ASP. Next, you'll see how to create report output using Active Server Pages.

ASP Reports

To replace a printed report with an Active Server Page, you need to take into consideration that you will be sending output that would appear on a printed report directly to the browser window. The advantage to this is that, if a user requires a hard copy of the report, he or she can simply print one out using the browser's Print function.

The following example report will display file and field information for a given library. (This example just goes through the steps of creating the ASP report, rather than comparing an RPG example to the Active Server Page.)

Every good report needs a good prompt screen. The prompt screen for this report is Rptprompt.asp, which is shown in Figure 4.13.

```
<!-- #include file="adovbs.inc" -->
<html>
<head><title>Library File Listing</title>
</head>
<body>
<form name=PROMOPT method=POST action="filelist.asp">
<table>
<tr><td>Select Library Name:</td><td><select name=lib>
<%
    Set conn=Server.CreateObject("ADODB.Connection")
    conn.open "DRIVER=Client Access ODBC Driver (32-bit); " & _
            "UID=user; PWD=secret; System=192.168.0.2;"

    Set rst=Server.CreateObject("ADODB.Recordset")
    rst.Open "SELECT DISTINCT TABLE_SCHEMA FROM QSYS2.SYSTABLES", _
    conn, adOpenKeyset
        rst.MoveFirst
        Do Until rst.EOF
            Response.Write "<option value='" & rst.Fields(0) & "'>"
            Response.Write rst.Fields(0) & "</option>"
            rst.MoveNext
        Loop
    rst.Close
    conn.Close
%>
```

Figure 4.13: This page acts as the prompt screen for an ASP report (part 1 of 2).

```
</select></td></tr>
<tr><td rowspan=2>
<input type=SUBMIT value="Display Report" NAME="Submit"></td></tr>
</table>
</form>
</body>
</html>
```

Figure 4.13: This page acts as the prompt screen for an ASP report (part 2 of 2).

This page performs a similar function to the HTML page in the previous example that prompts for a search item. The difference this time is that an Active Server Page creates a drop-down box containing the acceptable options for the field, in this case the library name. This eliminates the need for a validation outine because the user can only select valid options from the lists. An example of the output from this screen is displayed in Figure 4.14.

When the Display Report button is clicked, the value of the form variable Lib is submitted to the page Filelist.asp, which will create a "report" within the

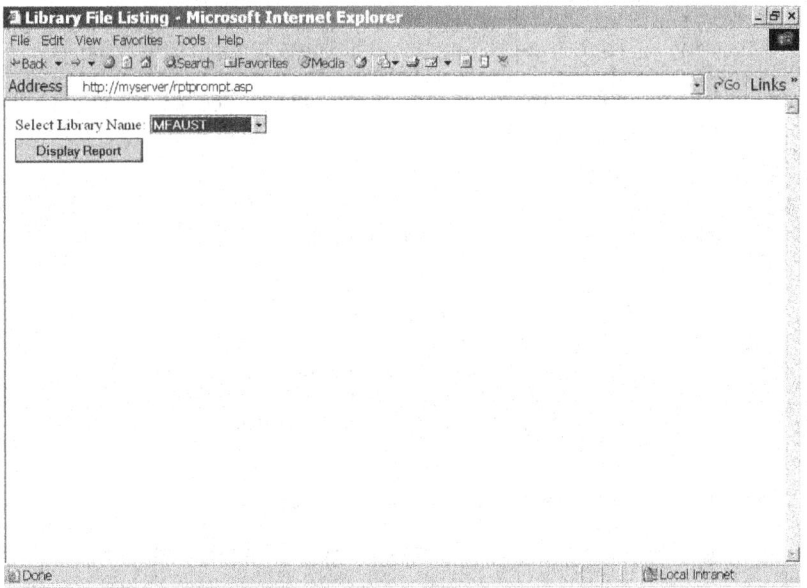

Figure 4.14: The ASP report's "prompt" screen looks like this in Internet Explorer.

Web browser. Again, the nice thing about building a report in the browser window is that the user can choose whether or not to obtain a hardcopy of the report using the browser's Print function.

The source for Filelist.asp is shown in Figure 4.15. This example contains many of the elements that would be found in an RPG report program, including level break control and detail time output. The data is read using a "SELECT" statement that selects the records from both the header file and the detail file at once (the SYSTABLES and SYSCOLUMNS files, respectively). This works in much the same way that an OPNQRYF statement can be used to combine data from multiple files in a CL program.

```
<!-- #include file="adovbs.inc" -->
<html>
<head><title>File Listing</title></head>
<STYLE type=text/css>
<FONT face="arial, helvetica" size=-3>

<!--
    BODY { BACKGROUND-ATTACHMENT: fixed; font-family:Verdana, Arial;
    color:black;font-size="x-small"; margin-right:0; }
    DIV { font-family:Verdana, arial, helvetica; color:black; }
    .Heading { font-size:12pt; line-height:12pt; color:black;
    font-weight:bold; }
    .Details { font-size:8pt; line-height:8pt; color:black;
        font-weight:regular; }
//-->
</STYLE>
<body>
<h3>Library:<%=Request.Form("Lib")%></h3>
<table>
<%
    'Create our connection object
    Response.write Session("conn")
    Set conn=Server.CreateObject("ADODB.Connection")
    conn.open "DRIVER=Client Access ODBC Driver (32-bit); " & _
            "UID=user; PWD=secret; System=192.168.0.2;"
    Lib= Request.Form("Lib")

    Set rst=Server.CreateObject("ADODB.Recordset")

' Retrieve our data.  All required data (header and detail)
```

Figure 4.15: This Active Server Page generates a report in the Web browser (part 1 of 2).

```
     ' retrieved with one statement
     Sql="SELECT B.TABLE_NAME, B.TABLE_TEXT, B.TABLE_TYPE,
         B.ROW_LENGTH," &_
         " A.COLUMN_NAME, A.COLUMN_TEXT, A.DATA_TYPE, A.LENGTH " & _
         "FROM QSYS2.SYSCOLUMNS A INNER JOIN QSYS2.SYSTABLES B ON " & _
         "A.TABLE_NAME=B.TABLE_NAME " & _
         "AND A.TABLE_SCHEMA=B.TABLE_SCHEMA " & _
         "WHERE B.TABLE_SCHEMA = '" & Lib & "' ORDER BY B.TABLE_NAME"


     rst.Open sql,conn,adOpenForwardOnly
     Do Until rst.EOF


     ' Equivalent to page headings
     ' The following lines perform level break logic
     If OldFile<>rst.Fields("TABLE_NAME") Then
     If OldFile<>"" Then Response.Write "</table></td></tr>"
     Response.write "<tr><th class=Heading>File Name</th>" & _
     "<th class=Heading>Description</th><th class=Heading>Type</th>" & _
     "<th class=Heading>Row Length</th></tr>"
     Response.Write "<tr>"
     For X=0 to 3
        Response.Write "<td>" & rst.Fields(X).Value & "</td>"
     Next
     Response.Write "</tr>"
     Response.write "<tr><td></td><td colspan=3><table><tr>" & _
     "<th class=Details>Field</th><th class=Details>Description</th>" & _
     "<th class=Details>Type</th><th class=Details>Length</th></tr>"
     End If
     'Write out detail lines
     response.Write "<tr>"
     For X=4 to 7
        Response.Write "<td>" & rst.Fields(X).Value & "</td>"
     Next
     response.Write "</tr>"
     'navigate to the next record
     OldFile=rst.Fields("TABLE_NAME")
     rst.MoveNext
     Loop


     rst.Close
%>
</tr>
</table>
</body>
</html>
```

Figure 4.15: This Active Server Page generates a report in the Web browser (part 2 of 2).

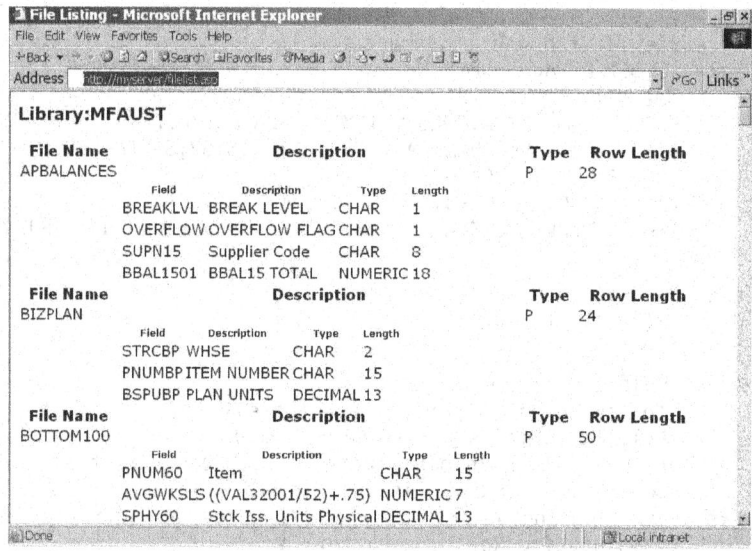

Figure 4.16: This page contains the output of the finished ASP report.

If the value of the Table_Name field differs from the value previously read, the "level header" is output in the form of an HTML table. The data for each detail line is output in its own HTML table. A sample of the resulting output is shown in Figure 4.16.

While this example contains simple file and field information, it could just as easily be a sales report, or an inventory report. The fact that you can perform complex calculations within an ASP's VBScript only adds to the number of reasons to consider Active Server Pages as a very attractive alternative for developing reports.

Summary

This chapter examined correlations between RPG operation codes and VBScript functions and statements. You saw how to convert both an interactive file-update application and a report-generation application into ASP applications. This information is probably best used to help familiarize yourself with the VBScript language, not as a tool for application conversion. The next two chapters examine creating ASP applications from the ground up.

5

ASP Order Entry

In previous chapters, you've seen relatively simple examples of how to use Active Server Pages. In this chapter, you'll go step-by-step through creating a basic order-entry application, complete with a shopping cart. The great part is that the iSeries database is the backbone for this ASP order-entry application. When this chapter is complete, you'll have a working ASP Web application.

The Building Blocks

The DDS source for all of the physical files in this example can be found in the companion code to this book. Before getting into creating the ASP code, I'd like to take a few minutes to examine each of these files and the function they serve. Table 5.1 lists the files used for the example and provides brief descriptions of the data they store.

For the purposes of the example, you need to create a library named ASPORDERS on your iSeries using the CRTLIB command, as shown here:

Table 5.1: The Files Used for the Order-entry Application

FileName	Description
CUSTMAST	Contains customer name, address and billing information.
ITEMMAST	Stores item information, including price, cost, and inventory data.
ORDERHDR	Contains the header-lever information for an order.
ORDERDTL	Stores the line details for an order.

```
CRTLIB LIB(ASPORDERS)
```

Next, you need to create some source physical files within the new library to hold the iSeries source required for the example. Use the following two commands to create these source physical files:

```
CRTSRCPF FILE(ASPORDERS/QRPGLESRC) RCDLEN(112)

CRTSRCPF FILE(ASPORDERS/QDDSSRC)
```

Once these files have been created, move the source for the physical files into QDDSSRC, and use the CRTPF command to create each of the files in Table 5.1, as shown below (replacing *filename* with the name of the file to be created):

```
CRTPF FILE(ASPORDERS/filename) SRCFILE(ASPORDERS/QDDSSRC)
```

The example application will use the ILE RPG program ORD001RG to generate a printed order-pick ticket when an order is generated. This program will be called from an ASP application upon completion of the order-entry process. The source for this program and the associated external printer-file DDS source (ORD001PR) can be found with the companion code to this book. Copy this source to the corresponding source physical files created earlier.

Now, create the printer file using the Create Printer File command, as shown below:

```
CRTPRTF FILE(ASPORDERS/ORD001PR) SRCFILE(ASPORDERS/QDDSSRC)
```

Next, compile the ILE RPG program using the Create Bound RPG command, as follows:

```
CRTBNDRPG PGM(ASOPRDERS/ORD001RP) SRCFILE(ASPORDERS/QRPGLESRC)
```

Once all of the work has been done on the iSeries, you're ready to start building ASP applications. You'll actually be creating three unique applications. The first two are administrative tools to maintain the item master file and customer master file. The third is the "shopping cart" application.

Item Master Maintenance

Before someone can order items through the order-entry application, the application needs a utility for adding, updating, and deleting items from the item master file. You saw a simple version of this in chapter 4. The application you'll be creating this time will include a little more information than that example. You'll also start adding a little more polish to the applications.

The first page of the item-maintenance application, Itemmaint1.asp, will read all of the items from the item master file and create a combo box using the <SELECT> HTML element. The code for Itemmaint1.asp is shown in Figure 5.1.

```
<HTML>
<HEAD>
<!-- #include file="adovbs.inc" -->
<TITLE>Item Maintenance</TITLE>
</HEAD>
<BODY BGCOLOR="#4682b4">
<TABLE cellSpacing=0 cellPadding=0 width="100%" align=center border=0>
<TR><TD>
   <TABLE cellSpacing=0 cellPadding=0 align=left border=0><TBODY>
   <TR HEIGHT=24><TD WIDTH=23><IMG src="leftsel.gif"></TD>
   <TD width=128 ALIGN=middle NOWRAP bgcolor=#ffff8c>
```

Figure 5.1: This page builds an HTML list box containing item numbers (part 1 of 2).

```
            <FONT COLOR="#4682b4" FACE=sans-serif size=-2
            style="COLOR: #4682b4">Item Maintenance</FONT></TD>
            <TD WIDTH=24><IMG src="rightsel.gif"></TD>
            <TD STYLE="CURSOR:HAND"
            ONCLICK="window.navigate('customermaint1.asp');">
                <TABLE CELLSPACING=0 CELLPADDING=0 BORDER=0><TR>
                <TD WIDTH=24><IMG src="leftunsel.gif"></TD>
                <TD width=196 ALIGN=middle NOWRAP bgcolor=#004080>
                <FONT COLOR="#4682b4" FACE=sans-serif size=-2
                style="COLOR: #ffff8c">Customer Maintenance</FONT></TD>
                <TD WIDTH=24><IMG src="rightunsel.gif"></TD></TR>
                </TABLE>
</TD></TR>
</TABLE>
</TD></TR><TR bgcolor=#ffff8c HEIGHT=480 VALIGN="TOP"><TD>
<FORM NAME="ITEMSEL" ACTION="ITEMMAINT2.ASP" METHOD=POST>
    <TABLE CELLSPACING=0 CELLPADDING=2 BORDER=0><TR HEIGHT=56
    VALIGN="BOTTOM">
    <TD></TD></td></td><TD><FONT COLOR="#4682b4" FACE=sans-serif
    size=-2 style="COLOR: #4682b4">Item Number:</FONT></TD>
    TD><SELECT NAME="itemnum" STYLE="WIDTH:120" MAXLENGTH=20>
<%
    'Define our ADO Connection object
    Set conn = Server.CreateObject("ADODB.Connection")
    conn.open "DRIVER=Client Access ODBC Driver (32-bit); " & _
        "UID=user; PWD=secret; System=192.168.0.2;"
    Set rst = Server.CreateObject("ADODB.Recordset")
    rst.Open "SELECT ITEMNO, ITDESC FROM ASPORDERS.ITEMMAST", Conn
    Do While Not rst.EOF
    Response.Write "<OPTION VALUE='" & rst.Fields(0) & "'>" & _
    rst.Fields(0) & " " & rst.Fields(1) & _
    "</OPTION>"
    rst.MoveNext
    Loop
    rst.Close
    conn.Close
%>
    </TD></TR><TR HEIGHT=56 VALIGN="BOTTOM"><TD> </TD>
    <TD ALIGN="CENTER">
    <INPUT TYPE="SUBMIT" NAME="CMD" VALUE="Update"></TD>
    <TD ALIGN="CENTER"><INPUT TYPE="SUBMIT" NAME="CMD"
    VALUE="New Item"></TD></TR>
    </TABLE></TD></TR>
</TABLE>
</BODY>
</HTML>
```

Figure 5.1: This page builds an HTML list box containing item numbers (part 2 of 2).

Figure 5.1 includes much more table formatting than in earlier examples. This formatting dresses up the application. The VBScript code uses techniques you've already seen to take data from the item master file and populate an HTML list box. It defines and opens the ADO Connection object (conn), then uses that connection to create the Recordset (rs). Next, it reads through each record in the Recordset and uses Response.Write to output an HTML <OPTION></OPTION> element for each record.

Note that the VALUE property on the <OPTION> tag is set to the value of the item number field, while the value displayed in the list box is a concatenation of the item number and item description. This allows the user to see both the item and the description, while only the item number is passed to the next page.

The list box created is contained within an HTML form that also contains "Update" and "New Item" SUBMIT buttons. An example of the output from this page is shown in Figure 5.2. Notice that this page contains two "pseudo-tabs," which is a common design in modern Web pages. In this example, it helps provide a simple user interface. The tabs themselves are cells in an HTML table

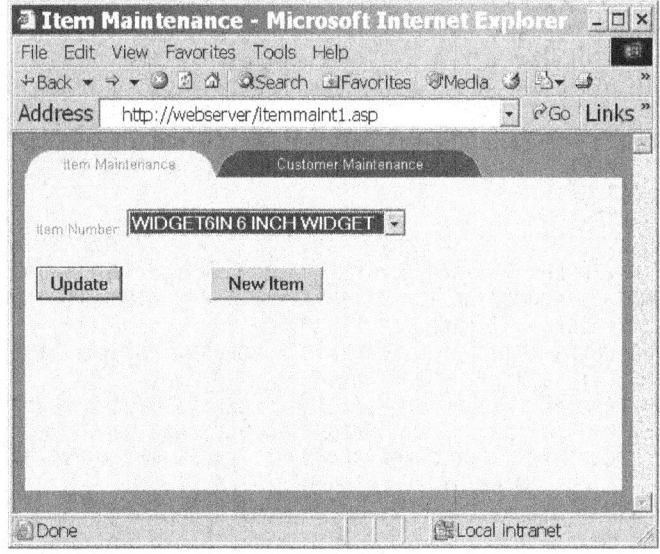

Figure 5.2: This is the first page of the item-maintenance application.

containing image files for the left and right sides of the tab and simple text to make up the tab heading.

When a user clicks the "Customer Maintenance" tab in Figure 5.2, the ONCLICK event fires, opening the Customermaint1.asp page. (You'll see this page later in this chapter.) When the user clicks either of the SUBMIT buttons, the form variables are sent to the Itemmaint2.asp page, the first part of which is shown in Figure 5.3.

```
<HTML>
<HEAD>
<!-- #include file="adovbs.inc" -->
<TITLE>Item Maintenance</TITLE>
</HEAD>
<BODY BGCOLOR="#4682b4">
<TABLE cellSpacing=0 cellPadding=0 width="100%" align=center border=0>
<TR><TD>
    <TABLE cellSpacing=0 cellPadding=0 align=left border=0>
    <TR HEIGHT=24><TD WIDTH=23><IMG src="leftsel.gif"></TD>
    <TD width=128 ALIGN=middle NOWRAP bgcolor=#ffff8c>
    <FONT COLOR="#4682b4"
    FACE=sans-serif size=-2 style="COLOR: #4682b4">Item Maintenance
    </FONT></TD><TD WIDTH=24><IMG src="rightsel.gif"></TD>
    <TD STYLE="CURSOR:HAND"
        ONCLICK="window.navigate('customermaint1.asp');">
        <TABLE CELLSPACING=0 CELLPADDING=0 BORDER=0><TR>
        <TD WIDTH=24><IMG src="leftunsel.gif"></TD>
        <TD width=196 ALIGN=middle NOWRAP bgcolor=#004080>
        <FONT COLOR="#4682b4" FACE=sans-serif size=-2
        style="COLOR: #ffff8c">Customer Maintenance</FONT></TD>
        <TD WIDTH=24><IMG src="rightunsel.gif"></TD></TR>
        </TABLE>
    </TD></TR>
    </TABLE>
</TD></TR><TR bgcolor=#ffff8c HEIGHT=280 VALIGN="TOP"><TD>
<FORM NAME="ITEMUPD" ACTION="ITEMMAINT3.ASP" METHOD=POST
onsubmit="return validate();">
    <TABLE CELLSPACING=0 CELLPADDING=2 BORDER=0 width=50%>
    <TR HEIGHT=56 VALIGN="BOTTOM">
    <TD ALIGN=left><TABLE CELLSPACING=0 CELLPADDING=2 BORDER=0
    width=50% ID="Table1"><TR HEIGHT=56 VALIGN="TOP">
    <TD ALIGN=left><FONT COLOR="#4682b4" FACE=sans-serif size=-2
    style="COLOR: #4682b4">Item Number:</FONT></TD>
    <%   'If in update mode, read in data.
```

Figure 5.3: This code will create the second page of the item-maintenance application (part 1 of 3).

```
    Mode=UCase(Request.Form("cmd"))
    If Mode="UPDATE" Then
        Set conn = Server.CreateObject("ADODB.Connection")
        conn.open "DRIVER=Client Access ODBC Driver (32-bit); " & _
        "UID=user; PWD=secret; System=192.168.0.2;"
        sql="SELECT * FROM ASPORDERS.ITEMMAST WHERE ITEMNO='" & _
        Request.Form("itemnum") & "'"
        Set rst = Server.CreateObject("ADODB.Recordset")
        rst.Open sql, Conn
    End If  %>
    <TD align=LEFT><INPUT TYPE=TEXT NAME="ITEM"
    <% If Mode="UPDATE" Then
        Response.Write " VALUE='" & rst.Fields(0) & "' DISABLED"
    End If  %>></TD><TD> </TD>
    <TD NOWRAP><FONT COLOR="#4682b4" FACE=sans-serif size=-2
    style="COLOR: #4682b4">Unit of Measure</font></TD>
    <TD ALIGN="CENTER"><INPUT TYPE=TEXT STYLE="WIDTH:36" NAME="UOM"
    <%  If Mode="UPDATE" Then
        Response.Write " VALUE='" & rst.Fields(5) & "'"
    End IF%> ID="Text2"></TD></TR>
</TABLE></td></tr>
    <TR HEIGHT=128 VALIGN="BOTTOM"><TD>
    <TABLE CELLPADDING=0 CELLSPACING=0 BORDER=0>
    <TR HEIGHT=64><TD> </TD><TD align=LEFT>
    <FONT COLOR="#4682b4" FACE=sans-serif size=-2
    style="COLOR: #4682b4">Description</font></TD>
    <TD COLSPAN=4 ALIGN="CENTER">
    <INPUT STYLE="WIDTH:320" TYPE=TEXT NAME="DESC"
    <% If Mode="UPDATE" Then
        Response.Write " VALUE='" & rst.Fields(1) & "'"
    End IF  %>></TD></TR><TR HEIGHT=64><TD> </TD><TD>
    <FONT COLOR="#4682b4" FACE=sans-serif size=-2
    style="COLOR: #4682b4">Price</font></TD>
    <TD ALIGN="CENTER">
    <INPUT STYLE="WIDTH:64; TEXT-ALIGN:RIGHT" TYPE=TEXT NAME="PRICE"
    <% If Mode="UPDATE" Then
        Response.Write " VALUE='" & rst.Fields(3) & "'"
    End IF%>></TD><TD><FONT COLOR="#4682b4" FACE=sans-serif size=-2
    style="COLOR: #4682b4">Cost</font></TD>
    <TD ALIGN="CENTER">
    <INPUT STYLE="WIDTH:64; TEXT-ALIGN:RIGHT" TYPE=TEXT NAME="COST"
    <% If Mode="UPDATE" Then
        Response.Write " VALUE='" & rst.Fields(4) & "'"
    End IF%>></TD></TR><TR VALIGN=TOP><TD> </TD><TD>
    <FONT COLOR="#4682b4" FACE=sans-serif size=-2
    style="COLOR: #4682b4">Weight</font></TD>
```

Figure 5.3: This code will create the second page of the item-maintenance application (part 2 of 3).

125

```
        <TD ALIGN="CENTER">
<INPUT STYLE="WIDTH:64; TEXT-ALIGN:RIGHT" TYPE=TEXT NAME="WEIGHT"
<% If Mode="UPDATE" Then
        Response.Write " VALUE='" & rst.Fields(2) & "'"
    End IF%> ID="Text1"></TD><TD>
<FONT COLOR="#4682b4" FACE=sans-serif size=-2 style="COLOR: #4682b4">
In Stock</font></TD><TD ALIGN="CENTER">
<INPUT STYLE="WIDTH:64; TEXT-ALIGN:RIGHT" TYPE=TEXT NAME="INSTOCK"
<% If Mode="UPDATE" Then
        Response.Write " VALUE='" & rst.Fields(6) & "'"
    End If %>> </TD></TR><TR><TD> </TD></TR><TR>
<TD> </TD><TD colspan=2><INPUT type=submit value=
<% if Mode="UPDATE" Then
        Response.Write "Update"
    Else
        Response.Write "Add"
    End If %> NAME="Submit"></TD><TD>
<% if Mode="UPDATE" Then
    Response.Write "<INPUT type=submit value='Delete' " & _
" NAME='Submit'>"
Else
    Response.Write " "
    End If%><TD colspan=3><INPUT type=button value="Cancel"
onclick="window.navigate('itemmaint1.asp');"></TD></TR>
</TABLE></TD></TR>
</TABLE></td></TR>
<TR HEIGHT=56 VALIGN="BOTTOM"></td></tr>
</TABLE>
```

Figure 5.3: This code will create the second page of the item-maintenance application (part 3 of 3).

When Itemmaint2.asp is loaded in a browser, it looks the same as Itemmaint1.asp. This gives the effect of adding fields to a single page and gives the application a uniform look. The page redisplays the item number selected on the previous display, along with other fields from the item master file. If the Update SUBMIT button was used, the field values are retrieved from the item master file using an ADO Connection and a Recordset that reads values from ITEMMAST. Otherwise, these fields will be blank when displayed.

This example embeds sections of code within HTML tags. In most cases, this code contains an If statement that determines whether or not to display a value in the field where the script is embedded. This reduces the overall size of the source by allowing the tags to be output without using the Response.Write method. However, this technique can make it more difficult to follow the flow of the page.

At the bottom of the form, three buttons appear. The text for the first button is determined by which SUBMIT button was selected on the first page. It can be either "Update" or "Add." In update mode, a second button labeled "Delete" is displayed by writing out an additional <INPUT> element whose type is SUBMIT. The Update (or Add) and Delete buttons will cause the values from the form fields on this page to be sent on to the next page, which will perform the file update/add/delete processing.

The third button is not a SUBMIT button, but just a simple command button. It is created by writing an <INPUT> element with a type of BUTTON. This button, labeled "Cancel," cancels any file updates through the use of the button's ONCLICK event. When the ONCLICK event fires, the Window.Navigate method is used to return to Itemmaint1.asp. This will abort any updates performed on the fields on Itemmaint2.asp.

Using Client-side Form Validation

You might have noticed the ONSUBMIT event defined on the <FORM> tag. The statement defined on this event is executed when a SUBMIT button is clicked, prior to actually submitting the form. In this case, the statement shown is "Return Validate()." When this code is executed, the JavaScript function Validate is executed. This function returns a value of either False or True. If False is returned, the form submission is cancelled, and the form is redisplayed. If True is returned, the form is submitted.

The second half of this page, which contains the Validate function, is shown in Figure 5.4. This client-side JavaScript function does some simple data validations to make sure that entries have been made in required fields, and that fields requiring a numeric entry contain only numbers.

You can refer to individual fields within a form using the following format:

```
document.formname.fieldname
```

```
<script language=javascript>
function validate() {
if (document.ITEMUPD.ITEM.value == '') {
  window.alert("Item Number Required!")
  window.alert("Unit of Measure Required!")
  return(false);}
if (document.ITEMUPD.UOM.value == '') {
  window.alert("Unit of Measure Required!")
  return(false);}
if (document.ITEMUPD.DESC.value == '') {
  window.alert("Item Description Required!")
  return(false);}
if (document.ITEMUPD.PRICE.value == '') {
  window.alert("Price Required!")
  return(false);}
if (document.ITEMUPD.COST.value == '') {
  window.alert("Cost Required!")
  return(false);}
if (document.ITEMUPD.WEIGHT.value == '') {
  window.alert("Weight Required!")
  return(false);}
var numtest = parseFloat(document.ITEMUPD.PRICE.value)
 if (isNaN(numtest)){
  window.alert("Price must be a number.")
  return(false);}
var numtest = parseFloat(document.ITEMUPD.COST.value)
 if (isNaN(numtest)){
  window.alert("Cost must be a number.")
  return(false);}
var numtest = parseFloat(document.ITEMUPD.WEIGHT.value)
 if (isNaN(numtest)){
  window.alert("Weight must be a number.")
  return(false);}
return(true);
}
</script>
</BODY>
</HTML>
```

Figure 5.4: This JavaScript function performs data validation on the form.

So, as shown in Figure 5.4, the value of the form's description field is referred to in JavaScript as follows:

```
document.ITEMUPD.DESC.value
```

Within the Validate function, if a field entry does not pass the validation check, an error message is displayed in a popup window using the window.alert JavaScript method, and the value False is returned. If all of the validations pass, True is returned, and control is passed on to the document defined on the form's ACTION property.

The output from Itemmaint2.asp is shown in Figure 5.5. When you display this screen in update mode, you'll notice that the Item Number field is grayed-out to prevent the user from modifying this field when updating the item.

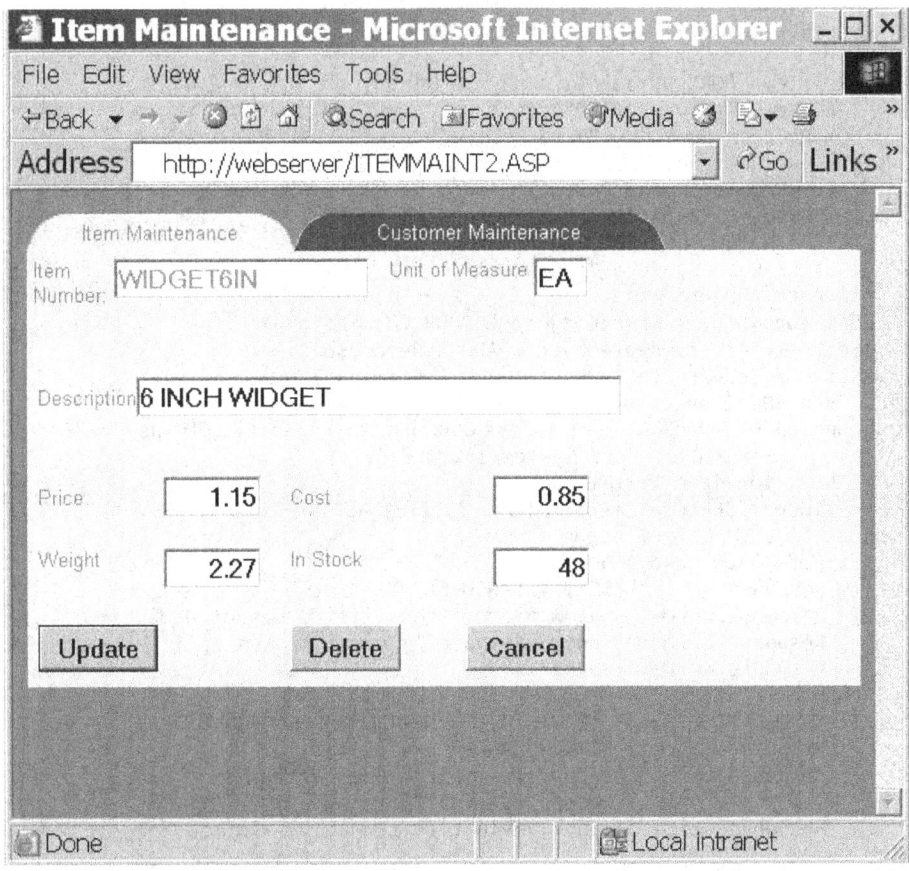

Figure 5.5: This is the second page of the item-maintenance example.

Maintenance File Update

When all form validations are passed on Itemmaint2.asp, the form field values
are passed to Itemmaint3.asp, which performs the actual file updates.
The source for this page is shown in Figure 5.6. This page reads the values
supplied on the ITEMUPD form in Itemmaint2.asp, and executes the update,
add, or delete.

```
<!-- #include file="adovbs.inc" -->
<%

'Retrieve mode using the submit button text
Mode=UCase(Request.Form("Submit"))

'Retrieve FORM variables into fields
ITEM=Request.Form("ITEM")
UOM=Request.Form("UOM")
DESC=Request.Form("DESC")
PRICE=Request.Form("PRICE")
COST=Request.Form("COST")
WEIGHT=Request.Form("WEIGHT")
INSTOCK=Request.Form("INSTOCK")
'Create ADO objects
Set conn=Server.CreateObject("ADODB.Connection")
Set rst=Server.CreateObject("ADODB.Recordset")
Set cmd=Server.CreateObject("ADODB.Command")
'Open ADO Connection
conn.open "DRIVER=Client Access ODBC Driver (32-bit); UID=user; " & _
        "PWD=secret; System=192.168.0.2;"
'Check for item record
rst.Open "SELECT * FROM ASPORDERS.ITEMMAST WHERE ITEMNO='" & _
        ITEM & "'", conn
If Mode="ADD" and NOT rst.eof Then
    Response.Write "<SCRIPT LANGUAGE=VBScript>"
    Response.Write "window.alert('Item Exists, Cannot Add');"
    Response.Write "window.navigate('itemmaint2.asp');"
    Response.Write "</SCRIPT>"
End If
If (Mode="UPDATE" or Mode="DELETE") and rst.eof Then
    Response.Write "<SCRIPT LANGUAGE=VBScript>"
    Response.Write "window.alert('Item Does Not Exist, " & _
                Cannot Update');"
    Response.Write "window.navigate('itemmaint2.asp');"
```

Figure 5.6: This page performs the file updates using ADO (part 1 of 3).

```
      Response.Write "</SCRIPT>"
      End If

'Generate Command Source based on the Mode
Select Case Mode
Case "UPDATE"
   cmd.CommandText="UPDATE ASPORDERS.ITEMMAST SET " & _
                  ITDESC=?, ITUOMS=?, ITPRIC=?, " & _
                  "ITCOST=?, ITWGHT=?, ITINST=? WHERE ITEMNO=?"
   Case "ADD"
   cmd.CommandText="INSERT INTO ASPORDERS.ITEMMAST(ITDESC, " & _
                  "ITUOMS, ITPRIC, ITCOST, ITWGHT, ITINST, " & _
                  "ITEMNO) VALUES(?, ?, ?, ?, ?, ?, ?)"
Case "DELETE"
   cmd.CommandText="DELETE FROM ASPORDERS.ITEMMAST WHERE ITEMNO=?"
End Select
cmd.ActiveConnection=conn

'Set Command Parameters based on the mode
If Mode="DELETE" Then
   cmd.Parameters(0)=ITEM
Else
   cmd.Parameters(0)=DESC
   cmd.Parameters(1)=UOM
   cmd.Parameters(2)=PRICE
   cmd.Parameters(3)=COST
   cmd.Parameters(4)=WEIGHT
   cmd.Parameters(5)=INSTOCK
   cmd.Parameters(6)=ITEM
End If

'Execute the command
cmd.Execute


'If errors returned, display message.
If conn.Errors.Count>0 Then
   errmsg=""
   For x=0 to conn.Errors.Count-1
      errmsg=errmsg & conn.Error(x) & chr(13)
   Next
   Response.Write "<SCRIPT LANGUAGE=Javascript>"
   Response.Write "window.alert('" & errmsg & "');"
   Response.Write "window.navigate('itemmaint2.asp');"
   Response.Write "</SCRIPT>"
End if
```

Figure 5.6: This page performs the file updates using ADO (part 2 of 3).

```
        'Close ADO object
        rst.Close
        conn.Close
        Response.Redirect "itemmaint1.asp"
    %>
```

Figure 5.6: This page performs the file updates using ADO (part 3 of 3).

Prior to executing the required "ACTION" SQL statement, an ADO Recordset object looks for the specified item in the database. If an Add operation is selected and the item already exists, or if an Update or Delete operation is selected and the item doesn't exist, an error is returned, and Itemmaint2.asp is redisplayed. This error is displayed by writing out a client-side script using the HTML <SCRIPT></SCRIPT> element. First, window.alert displays the error in a message box, and then window.navigate redirects the user back to Itemmaint2.asp.

If this final validation check is passed, a Command object performs the actual file updates. This is done by using Response.Write to create the client-side JavaScript code, display the message, and redisplay Itemmaint2.asp. The ADODB.Command object creates an SQL statement to perform the desired file operation. The Select Case statement is used with the value of the variable Mode to determine which statement to use.

After performing the Execute method on the Command object, this same technique generates JavaScript code to display a message notifying the user that the updates are complete. This script then redirects the browser to Itemmaint1.asp, allowing the user to maintain more item master records.

Customer Master Maintenance

The second "tab" on the maintenance screen directs the user to Customermaint1.asp, as shown in Figure 5.7. This page is the first of three pages used to maintain the customer master file. These pages operate in almost the same manner as the item-maintenance function discussed in the previous section. The code for these three pages can be found with the companion code to this book.

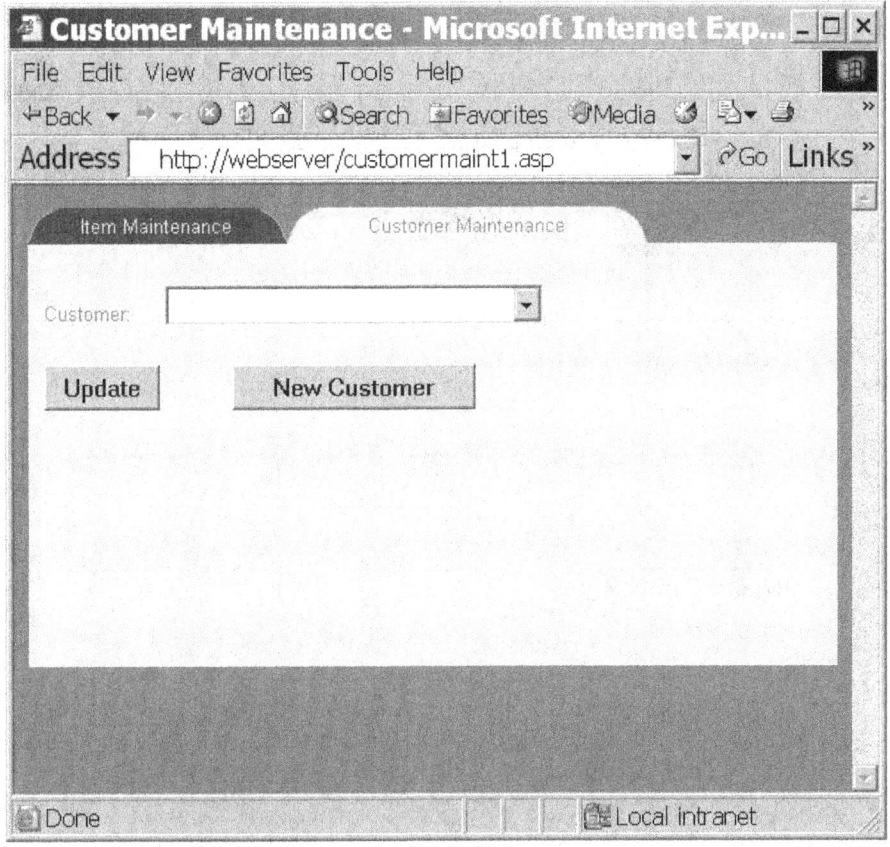

Figure 5.7: This is the first page of the customer-master maintenance function.

Notice that the Item Maintenance tab now appears to be in the back, and the Customer Maintenance tab appears in the front. This technique allows you to give the effect of a single user interface even though the application is made up of multiple pages. Figure 5.8 shows the second page of this tab, Customermaint2.asp.

As with the item master maintenance, this page allows the user to add, modify, or delete records in the customer master file. When the user clicks the New Customer button, the value of the customer number field for the new customer is determined by reading the highest customer number currently in the file, using an ADO Recordset. This value is then incremented by one to arrive at the new

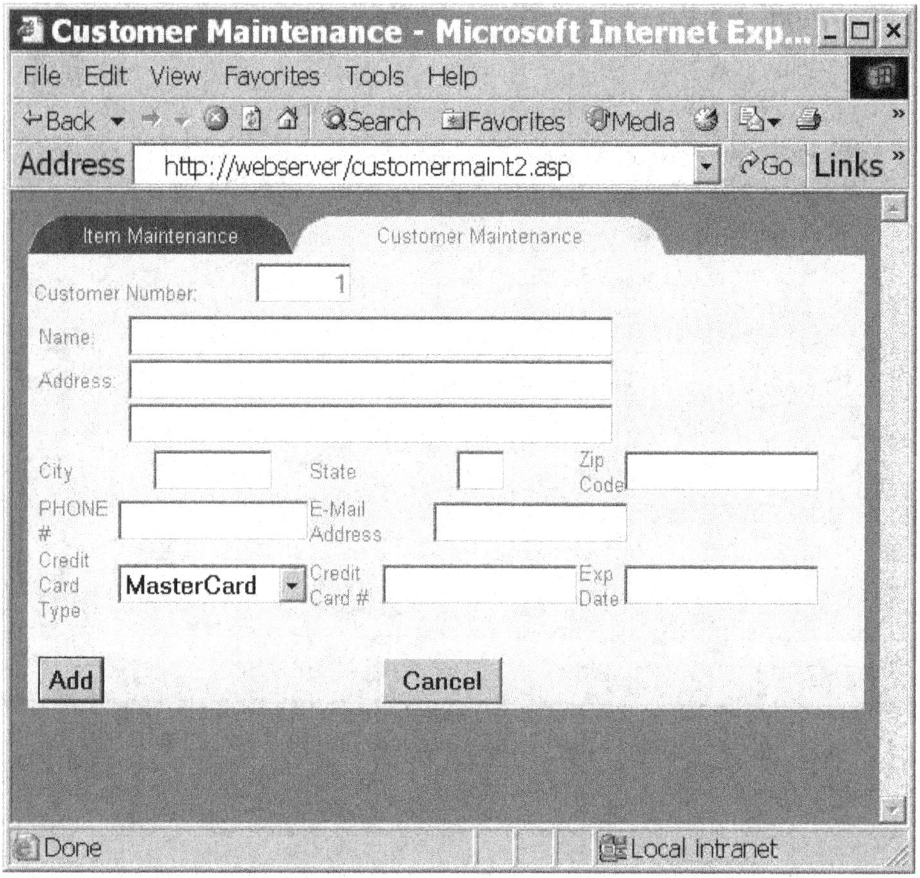

Figure 5.8: *Customer master data is modified within this page.*

customer number. Alternatively, you could use an ASP Application variable to store and retrieve this next-up value, but you would lose the Application variable any time that the Web server was restarted. The remaining entries made on this form are passed to Customermaint3.asp, which performs the same validations and updates as Itemmaint3.asp.

These two file-maintenance applications are used to prepare data for an ASP order-entry application. Realistically, these applications could be created on the iSeries, since that's where the data resides. In a full-blown order-entry system, you would probably need many other setup files, but for the purposes of this example, these two files are enough.

The Order-entry Application

The order-entry application will allow a user to create header and detail order information. At any point during the process of entering an order, a user may, intentionally or accidentally, exit the application. If partial order data has already been written to the order file when this occurs, erroneous order information could be created.

If you were writing this application on the iSeries, you might solve this problem by creating a work file to hold the data temporarily, or store it in a subfile until the order was complete. In an Active Server Page, you have another option: store the data temporarily in Session variables. Session variables provide an ideal solution here because they are deleted automatically when the session is closed.

The first page of the order-entry application displays a list of items in the form of a catalog. The ASP portion of the source for this page, Catalog.asp, is shown in Figure 5.9.

```
<% 'Display Item Catalog
' Define number of lines per page
set conn = Server.CreateObject("ADODB.Connection")
conn.open "DRIVER=Client Access ODBC Driver (32-bit); " & +
        "UID=user; PWD=secret; System=192.168.0.2;"

lnperPg = 10  ' This value identifies the number of lines per page.

' set up a query to get the count, and another to get the data
countSQL = "SELECT count(ITEMNO) FROM MFAUST.ITEMMAST"
dataSQL = "SELECT ITEMNO, ITDESC, ITPRIC, ITINST FROM MFAUST.ITEMMAST " & _
        "ORDER BY ITEMNO"

' Determine the number of records using the countSQL statement
set rs=Server.CreateObject("ADODB.Recordset")
```

Figure 5.9: This code generates the catalog (part 1 of 4).

135

```
rs.Open countSQL,conn
cnt = clng(rs(0))
rs.close

' If no records, display message to the browser.
if cnt < 1 then
   Response.Write "No items in catalog."
   Response.End
else
   if cnt = 1 then lnperpg = 1
   pages = clng(cnt/lnperpg)
   if cnt/lnperpg > pages then
      pages = pages + 1
   end if
   ' what page are we on?
   page = clng(request.querystring("page"))
Response.Write "<tr><td class=menu colspan=2>"
If Pages>1 Then
   Response.Write "Page: "
   For x=1 to pages
   If x<>page Then
      Response.Write "<a href='catalog.asp?page=" & x & _
                     "'>" & x & "</a> "
   Else
         Response.Write x & " "
   End If
   Next
End if

Response.Write "</td>"
Response.Write "<td class=menu colspan=2 align=right>"
if page>1 then response.Write "<A HREF='catalog.asp?page=" & page-1 & _
"'>Previous</a> "
if pages>page then response.Write "<A HREF='catalog.asp?page=" & page+1 & _
"'>Next</a>"
Response.Write "</td></tr>"
If pages>1 then response.Write "<tr><td colspan=4><hr></td></tr>"
   if page <= 1 then
      page = 1
   elseif page > pages then
      page = pages
   end if
   cp = page
end if
' move to first record for the current screen
if pages > 1 then
```

Figure 5.9: This code generates the catalog (part 2 of 4).

```
      startrecord = (clng(page-1) * lnperpg) + 1
end if
' Open database
rs.Open dataSQL,conn,adOpenKeyset

rs.move(startrecord-1)

' Read from the database the number of records for a page or until EOF
' display values within the table

for x = 1 to lnperpg
   if not rs.eof then
      Response.Write "<TR VALIGN=TOP>"
      Set fso=Server.CreateObject("Scripting.FileSystemObject")
      If fso.FileExists("images\" & trim(rs.Fields("ITEMNO").Value) & _
                  ".jpg") Then
      FileName="images\" & trim(rs.Fields("ITEMNO").Value) & ".jpg"
      Else
      FileName="images\noimage.jpg"
      End If

      'Output form for each item in the catalog
      Response.Write "<form name=ord" & startrecord+x & _
                  " method=POST action='shoppingcart.asp'>"
      Response.Write "<td colspan=3 ALIGN=LEFT><font size=-1><b>" & _

             rs.Fields(0) & "</b><BR>"
      Response.Write rs.Fields(1) & "<INPUT TYPE=HIDDEN " & _
             "NAME=ITEM VALUE='" & rs.Fields(0) & "'><BR><br>"
      Response.Write "<INPUT TYPE=TEXT NAME=QTY STYLE='text-" & _
                  "align:right; width:50' value=1> "
      Response.Write "<INPUT TYPE=SUBMIT NAME=SUBMIT VALUE='" & _
         "Add to Cart'></td>"
      Response.Write "<TD WIDTH=10% ALIGN=right><IMG BORDER=1 " & _
         " SRC='" & FileName & "'></td></TR>"
      Response.Write "<TR><td><b>Price:</b></td><td align=right>" & _
                  "<font size=-1>" & FormatNumber(rs.Fields(2),2) &_
                  "</TD>"
      Response.Write "<td align=right><b>Availability:</b></td>"
      Response.Write "</form>"
      If CINT(rs.Fields("ITINST").Value)>5 Then
         Response.Write "<TD NOWRAP ALIGN=LEFT>" & _
                     "<font size=-1 color=blue>In Stock</TD>"
      Else
         If CINT(rs.Fields("ITINST").Value)>0 Then
            Response.Write "<TD NOWRAP ALIGN=LEFT>" & _
```

Figure 5.9: This code generates the catalog (part 3 of 4).

137

```
              "<font size=-1 color=Goldenrod>Only " & _
              rs.Fields("ITINST") & " left..Order Now!</TD>"
         Else

            Response.Write "<TD NOWRAP ALIGN=LEFT><font " & _
                           "size=-1 color=Red>Out of Stock</TD>"
         End If
      End If
   response.Write"</TR><tr><td colspan=4> <HR width='100%' SIZE='2' " &_
       " COLOR='ROYALBLUE'></td></tr>"
   rs.MoveNext
   response.flush
   End If
next
Response.Write "</tr><tr><td colspan=3>"

'Output Page navigation links

If Pages>1 Then
   Response.Write "Page: "
   For x=1 to pages
   If x<>page Then
      Response.Write "<a href='catalog.asp?page=" & x & _
                     "'>" & x & "</a> "
   Else
      Response.Write x & " "
   End If
   Next
End if
Response.Write "</td>"
Response.Write "<td colspan=2 align=right>"
if page>1 then response.Write "
<A HREF='catalog.asp?page=" & page-1 & _
                        "'>Previous</a> "
if pages>page then
   response.Write "<A HREF='catalog.asp?page=" & page+1 & _
              "'>Next</a>"
   Response.Write "</td></tr>"

' close the Recordset and connection
rs.close: set rs = nothing
conn.close: set conn = nothing
%>
```

Figure 5.9: This code generates the catalog (part 4 of 4).

This page will display 10 items per page using the same technique discussed in chapter 4 for simulating a subfile display. It keeps a count of the number of lines per page, the current start line, and the current page. An ADO Recordset whose SQL statement uses the "COUNT(*)" operator determines the number of records in the table. This value is divided by the number of lines per page to determine the total number of pages. This information is used to write out hyperlinks, with which the user can navigate to a specific page. Within these hyperlinks, the page number is passed through a Querystring variable. When the "page" Querystring value is present, it is multiplied by the lines per page to determine the starting record number. This value is used with the rs.Move operation to position the Recordset to the required record.

As the application reads through the item file, it generates the catalog display. This example uses the FileSystemObject ActiveX control to check for the existence of an image file whose name is the item number with an extension of ".jpg." If that file exists, it is displayed as part of the catalog. If there is no image file for a given item, an image file that displays the message "NO IMAGE FOUND" is shown in its place.

Each item is displayed within its own HTML form. This allows for the inclusion of an <INPUT> element for entering order quantity and a "Buy Now" SUBMIT button for adding the item to the shopping cart. The output from this application is shown in Figure 5.10.

Notice the menu displayed along the left side of the page in Figure 5.10. The code that generates this menu is contained in the include file Sidebar.inc. An *include file* allows you to place common page components like this within a single source, and include this source in any pages requiring the menu. This helps simplify the application design. The source for Sidebar.inc is shown in Figure 5.11.

Sidebar.asp's Checkout and Show Cart buttons are only displayed if there are items in the shopping cart. The Continue Shopping button displays Catalog.asp, so that button does not appear when Catalog.asp is displayed.
The Contact button, however, is always displayed. When clicked, it uses a MAILTO link along with a specified e-mail address to launch the user's e-mail client.

139

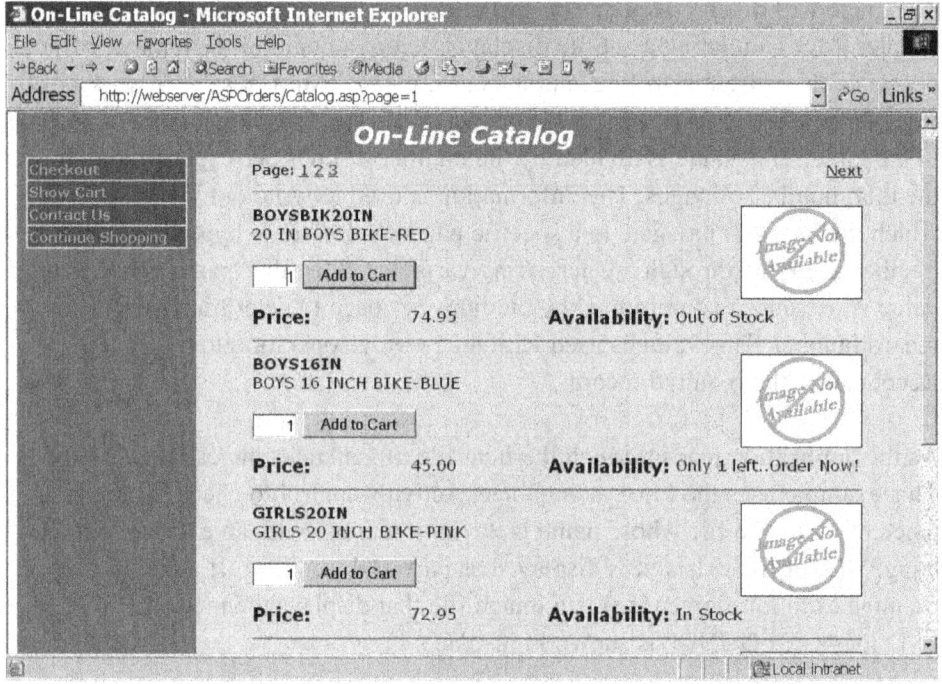

Figure 5.10: This ASP page is used by the shopping-cart application.

Since Sidebar.asp is included in all of the pages for the shopping-cart application, you need to determine which page called it, to know which buttons to display. This is done by using Request.ServerVariable("URL") to return the name of the page that included Sidebar.asp.

```
<TABLE WIDTH=90% bgcolor="Khaki" BORDER="0" CELLSPACING="2"
CELLPADDING="1">
<%  If IsNull(Session("Cart")) Then
        Response.Write "<A href='checkout.asp'>
        <TR CLASS=MENU BGCOLOR='DarkSlateBlue' onmouseover='mOvr();'
        onmouseout='mOut();'> <TD>Checkout</TD></TR></A>"
        Response.Write "<A href='shoppingcart.asp'><TR CLASS=MENU
        BGCOLOR='DarkSlateBlue' onmouseover='mOvr();' onmouseout='mOut();'>
        <TD>Show Cart</TD></TR></A>"
    End If %>
```

Figure 5.11: This code generates a menu along the side of the Web page in Figure 5.10 (part 1 of 2).

140

```
<A HREF='mailto:me@mail.com'><TR CLASS=MENU BGCOLOR='DarkSlateBlue'
onmouseover='mOvr();' onmouseout='mOut();'>
<TD>Contact Us</TD></TR></A>
<% If Request.Servervariables("URL")<>"/catalog.asp" Then
Response.Write "<A HREF='catalog.asp'><TR CLASS=MENU
BGCOLOR='DarkSlateBlue' onmouseover='mOvr();' onmouseout='mOut();'>" &_
"<TD>Continue Shopping</TD></TR></A>" %>
</TABLE>
```

Figure 5.11: This code generates a menu along the side of the Web page in Figure 5.10 (part 2 of 2).

When a user selects one of the "Buy Now" SUBMIT buttons, the values of the ITEM, QTY, and PRICE fields are all passed to the page Shoppingcart.asp. This page adds the selected item to the shopping cart, and then displays all of the items currently in the shopping cart. This same page will be displayed when a user selects Show Cart from the sidebar menu. The ASP portion of Shoppingcart.asp is shown in Figure 5.12.

The form that displays the items in the cart can also be used to modify the quantity or remove items from the cart. The ACTION attribute of the <FORM> tag refers back to this same page. When the page is loaded, the values of the SUBMIT buttons from the form on Catalog.asp and the SUBMIT buttons on this page are read to determine which button was clicked.

Notice that the form variables CONTI.X, PROCE.X, and RECALC.X are read. These variables represent the horizontal position of the mouse cursor within the image <INPUT> elements used as SUBMIT buttons for the form. If the X property has a value, the image was clicked. This is how the code determines which of the buttons was clicked.

```
<% Dim item, qty , Cart, numLines
'Read form variables
item = Request.Form("item")
qty = Request.Form("qty")
desc = Request.Form("desc")
```

Figure 5.12: This source is used to maintain and display the shopping cart (part 1 of 4).

```
price = Request.Form("price")
redim Cart(4,999)
'Read in session variables
Cart = Session("Cart")
numLines = Session("numLines")
'If quantity is zero or blank, display error.
If qty <> "" AND qty < 1 then
    Response.Redirect "error.asp?msg=" & Server.URLEncode
("Please enter at least 1 as number of items you wish to order.")
End if
If item <> "" Then
' Add item to cart array
   If numLines < 999 Then
      numLines = numLines + 1
      Session("numLines") = numLines
      Cart(3,numLines) = qty
      Cart(4,numLines) = price
      Session("Cart") = Cart
      Session("numLines") = numLines
   End If
Else
   Dim strCmd
   If Request.Form("CONTI.X")>0 Then
      strCmd="CONTI"
   End If
   If Request.Form("PROCE.X")>0 Then
      strCmd="PROCE"
   End If
   If Request.Form("RECALC.X")>0 Then
      strCmd="RECAL"
   End If
   If strCmd<>"" and strCmd<> "RECAL" Then
      Select Case strCmd
      Case "CONTI"              'continue shopping
         Response.Redirect "catalog.asp"
      Case "PROCE"              'proceed to checkout
         error=false
         Response.Redirect "login.asp"
      End Select
   Else
   ' recalculate the cart contents
      If strCmd="RECAL" Then
         call recalcCart()
      End If
   End if
'end if for updating or inserting new item in Cart
```

Figure 5.12: This source is used to maintain and display the shopping cart (part 2 of 4).

```
End If
' Recalculate order totals and cart lines
sub recalcCart()
' look for changed Line quantities
numLines=Session("numLines")
For i = 1 To numLines
   Dim tquantity
   tquantity = Request.Form("qty" & Cstr(i))
   if isempty(tquantity) OR (tquantity = "") then
      tquantity = 0
   elseif (tquantity < 0) OR (isnumeric(tquantity)=false) then
      tquantity = 0
   end if
   Cart(3,i) = CInt(tquantity)
Next
' Look for lines that are deselected or lines with zero quantities
and condense array.

For i = 1 to numLines
   confirm = Request.Form("sel" & CStr(i))
   qnty = Cart(2,i)
   If confirm = "" OR qnty = "0" Then
      numLines = numLines - 1
      For x = 1 to UBound(Cart,1)
         Cart(x,i) = ""
      Next
      n = i
      while n < UBound(Cart,2)
         For x = 1 to UBound(Cart,1)
            Cart(x,n) = Cart(x,n + 1)
            Cart(x,n + 1) = ""
         Next
         n = n + 1
      wend
   End If
Next
   Session("Cart") = Cart
   Session("numLines") = numLines
end sub
if numLines = 0  then
   Response.Write "<h3>Your shopping cart is empty.</h3>"
   Response.Write "<p><a href='catalog.asp'>" & _
   "Continue shopping.</a></p>"
else
   Response.Write "<FORM Name=ShopCart action='shoppingcart.asp' " &_
   "method='POST' onsubmit='return valid(ShopCart);'>"
```

Figure 5.12: This source is used to maintain and display the shopping cart (part 3 of 4).

```
      Response.Write  "<table border=0 cellPadding=3 cellSpacing=2 " & _
      "width='100%'>"
      Response.Write "<tr bgColor=darkblue>"
      Response.Write "<td><FONT color=white>Item</FONT></td>"
      Response.Write "<td><FONT color=white>Description</FONT></td>"
      Response.Write "<td><FONT color=white>Quantity</FONT></td>"
      Response.Write "<td><FONT color=white>Unit Price</FONT></td>"
      Response.Write "<td><FONT color=white>Total</FONT></td></tr>"
      Response.Write "<input type=HIDDEN name='numLines' " & _
      "value="&numLines&">"
      Dim cartTot, i
      cartTot = 0
   For i = 1 to numLines
      Response.Write "<tr bgColor=navajowhite>"
      Response.Write "<td><input name=sel"& Cstr(i)& _
      " type=checkbox value='yes' checked>" & _
      Cart(1,i) &"</td>"
      Response.Write "<td>" & Cart(1,i) & "</td>"
      Response.Write "<td><input type=HIDDEN name='item" & _
      cstr(i) & "' VALUE='" & Cart(1,i) & "'>"
      Response.Write "<input type='text' name='qty"& CStr(i) & _
      "' value='" & Cart(3,i) &"' size=3><br></td>"
      Response.Write "<td>" & FormatCurrency(Cart(4,i),2) & "</td>"
      Response.Write "<td>"&FormatCurrency(Cart(4,i)*Cart(3,i),2)&_
      "</td>"
      Response.Write "</tr>"
      cartTot = cartTot + (Cart(4,i) * Cart(3,i))
   Next
      Response.Write "<tr>"
      Response.Write "<td></td><td></td><td></td>"
      Response.Write "<td bgColor=darkblue><font color=white>" & _
      "Total</font></td>"
      Response.Write "<td bgColor=lightgoldenrodyellow>" & _
      FormatCurrency(cartTot,2) & "</td>"
      Response.Write "</tr>"
      Response.Write "</table>"
      Response.Write "<BR><BR><a href='addprod.asp?action=CONTI'>" & _
      "<INPUT src='images/keepshpn.gif' name='CONTI' type='image'" & _
      " value='continue'></a>"
      Response.Write "<input src='images/recalc.gif' name='RECALC'" & _
      " type='image' value='Recalculate'>"
      Response.Write "<input src='images/checkbutn.gif' name='PROCE'"&_
      " type='image' value='Checkout'></a>"
      Response.Write "</form>"
   End If
   %>
```

Figure 5.12: This source is used to maintain and display the shopping cart (part 4 of 4).

When the Recalculate button is selected, and the check box next to a given item in the cart is unchecked, that item is removed from the cart. Any changes in item quantity are also reflected on the screen. At the same time, any items removed from the order are taken off the screen, and those lines are taken out of the total. These actions are done by reading through the variables that relate to the check box and to the quantity field associated with each item in the cart.

The shopping cart itself is actually a multi-dimensional array stored in a Session variable. This technique provides easy access to the order data without adding the overhead of creating ADO objects until the order is complete. The sample output from Shoppingcart.asp is shown in Figure 5.13. Notice that the sidebar on the left side of the screen shows the Continue Shopping button.

When the user clicks the Checkout button on Figure 5.13, the application navigates to Login.html, shown in Figure 5.14. This page allows the user to log into his or her account. The user can enter an e-mail address and password and click Login, or click the Create Account button, which allows the user to enter additional customer information. This page contains strictly HTML code, since it only displays a static HTML form.

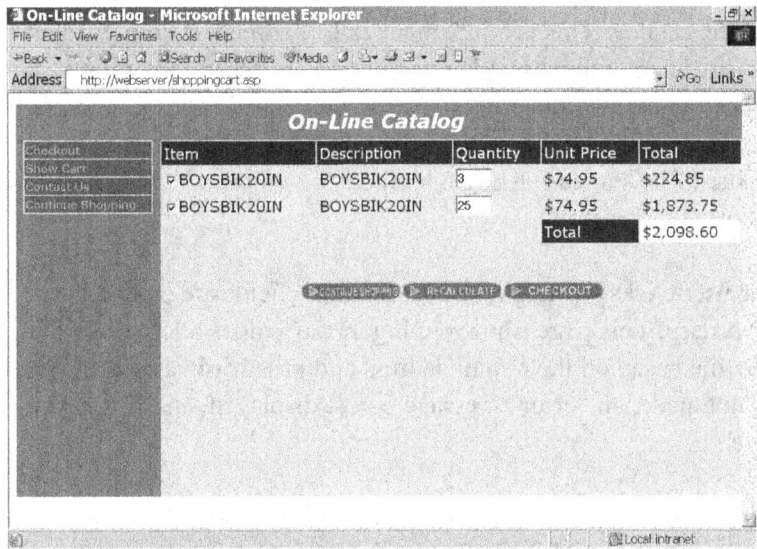

Figure 5.13: The contents of the shopping cart are displayed in this page.

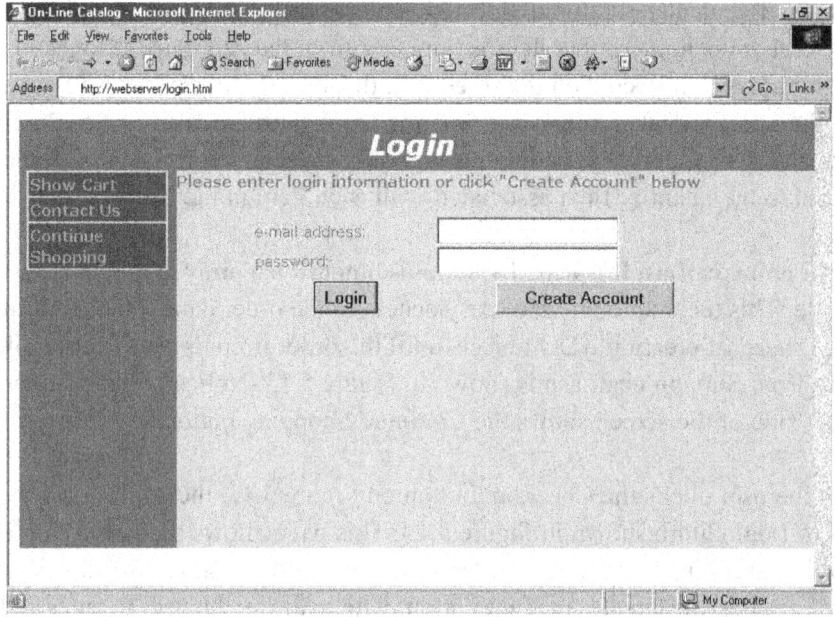

Figure 5.14: This HTML page allows a customer to log in.

You might be wondering why the user isn't required to log in prior to browsing the catalog. This is a judgment call. If someone simply wants to browse the catalog without making any purchases, there's no point in forcing him or her to log in. On the other hand, if you wanted to restrict access to the catalog to only approved customers, it would make more sense to have them log in at the start. The source for Login.html can be found with the companion code to this book.

When the user clicks the Login button, the form fields are passed to Validateuser.asp. This page, shown in Figure 5.15, does a lookup in the CUSTMAST file based on the e-mail address and password values entered. If a match is not made, an "error" message box is displayed, and Login.html is redisplayed.

When Validateuser.asp finds a matching customer record, the customer number from that record is placed in the Session variable Custnumber, and the page is redirected to Processord.asp.

```
<% ' Define connection object
   set conn = Server.CreateObject("ADODB.Connection")
   conn.open "DRIVER=Client Access ODBC Driver (32-bit); " & _
             "UID=user; PWD=secret; System=192.168.0.2;"

' Determine if the email address/password combination are valid
   set rs=Server.CreateObject("ADODB.Recordset")
   rs.Open "SELECT * FROM ASPORDERS.CUSTMAST WHERE EMAIL='" & _
   Request.Form("email") & "' AND WEBPWD='" & _
   Request.Form("pass") & "' ",conn

'If no matching record found, display message and redirect to login
page
If rs.EOF Then
   ' close the Recordset and connection, display error and redirect
   rs.close: set rs = nothing
   conn.close: set conn = nothing
   Response.Write "<SCRIPT LANGUAGE='Javascript'>" & Chr(13)
   Response.Write "window.alert('Invalid account information');"&Chr(13)
   Response.Write "window.navigate('login.html');" & chr(13)
   Response.Write "</SCRIPT>" & Chr(13)
Else
   ' close the Recordset and connection and redirect
   Session("Custnumber")=rs.fields("CUSTNO")
   rs.close: set rs = nothing
   conn.close: set conn = nothing
   Response.Redirect "processord.asp"
End If
%>
```

Figure 5.15: This page validates the user login information.

If the user selects the Create Account button from the login screen, Createaccount.html is displayed instead of Validateuser.asp. The output from Createaccount.html is shown in Figure 5.16. This page is similar to the page used to maintain customer account information shown in Figure 5.8. The exception is that the customer number is not displayed. (Note that this application doesn't include any credit-card validation logic because, if it were required, it would most likely be handled by third-party software.)

The information from this page is submitted to Createcust.asp. This page is very similar to Customermaint3.asp, discussed earlier in this chapter. The source for this page is shown in Figure 5.17.

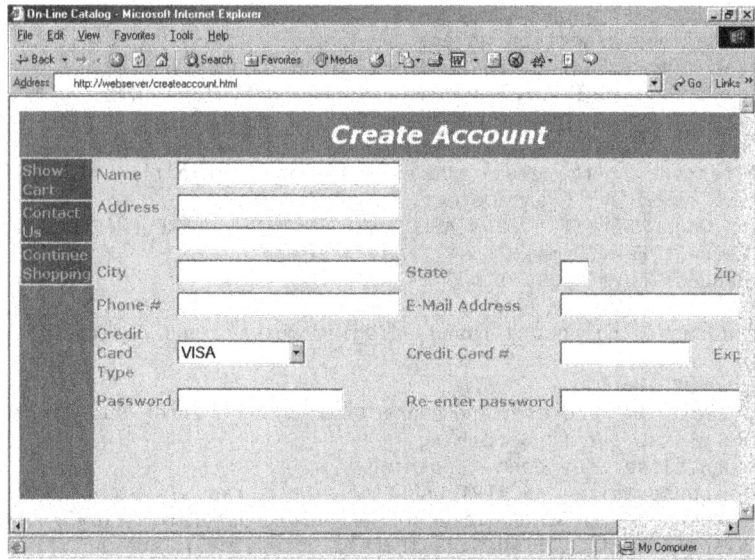

Figure 5.16: This page allows a user to create account information.

```
<!-- #include file="adovbs.inc" -->
<% 'Retrieve FORM variables into fields
   NAME=Request.Form("NAME")
   ADD1=Request.Form("ADD1")
   ADD2=Request.Form("ADD2")
   CITY=Request.Form("CITY")
   STATE=Request.Form("STATE")
   ZIP=Request.Form("ZIP")
   EMAIL=Request.Form("EMAIL")
   PHONE=Request.Form("PHONE")
   CCTYPE=Request.Form("CCTYPE")
   CCARD=Request.Form("CCARD")
   EXPDT=Request.Form("EXPDT")
   PASS=Request.Form("PASS")
   'Create ADO objects
   Set conn=Server.CreateObject("ADODB.Connection")
   Set rst=Server.CreateObject("ADODB.Recordset")
   Set cmd=Server.CreateObject("ADODB.Command")
   'Open ADO Connection
   conn.open "DRIVER=Client Access ODBC Driver (32-bit); " & _
             "UID=user; PWD=secret; System=192.168.0.2;"
```

Figure 5.17: This Active Server Page writes out the new customer-account information (part 1 of 3).

```
'Retrieve last used customer number
   sql="SELECT MAX(CUSTNO) FROM ASPORDERS.CUSTMAST "
   Set rst = Server.CreateObject("ADODB.Recordset")
   rst.Open sql, Conn

   'Increment last customer by one
   CUSTNO=rst.Fields(0).Value + 1
   If IsNull(CUSTNO) Or CUSTNO="" Or CUSTNO=0 then  CUSTNO=1

   'Generate Command Source based on the Mode

   cmd.CommandText="INSERT INTO ASPORDERS.CUSTMAST(CUSNAM, CUADD1, " & _
      "CUCITY, CUADD2, CUSTAB, CUZIPC, CUPHON, EMAIL, CCNO, " & _
      "CCTYPE, CCEXPR, WEBPW, CUSTNO) " & _
      "VALUES(?, ?, ?, ?, ?, ?, ?, ?, ?, ?, ?, ?)"

   cmd.ActiveConnection=conn
   'Set Command Parameters
   cmd.Parameters(0)=NAME
   cmd.Parameters(1)=ADD1
   cmd.Parameters(2)=ADD2
   cmd.Parameters(3)=CITY
   cmd.Parameters(4)=STATE
   cmd.Parameters(5)=LEFT(ZIP,9)
   cmd.Parameters(6)=LEFT(PHONE,10)
   cmd.Parameters(7)=EMAIL
   cmd.Parameters(8)=CCARD
   cmd.Parameters(9)=CCTYPE
   cmd.Parameters(10)=EXPDT
   cmd.Parameters(11)=PASS
   cmd.Parameters(12)=CUSTNO

   'Execute the command
   cmd.Execute

   'If errors returned, display message.
   If conn.Errors.Count>0 Then
      errmsg=""
      For x=0 to conn.Errors.Count-1
         errmsg=errmsg & conn.Error(x) & chr(13)
      Next
      Response.Write "<SCRIPT LANGUAGE=VBScript>"
      Response.Write "window.alert('" & errmsg & "');"
      Response.Write "window.navigate('creataccount.html');"
      Response.Write "</SCRIPT>"
   End if
```

Figure 5.17: This Active Server Page writes out the new customer-account information (part 2 of 3).

149

```
    'Close ADO objects
    rst.Close
    conn.Close
    Session("custnum")=CUSTNO
    Response.Redirect "processord.asp"
%>
```

Figure 5.17: This Active Server Page writes out the new customer-account information (part 3 of 3).

This page uses an SQL "INSERT INTO" statement to add the customer information to the customer master table. Once this information is written out, the customer number for the new account is moved to the Session variable Custnum, and control is redirected to Processord.asp.

The Processord.asp page reads the order information from the shopping-cart Session variable, along with the customer number from the Custnum Session variable, and writes out the order header and detail lines using ADO Command objects. The source for this page is shown in Figure 5.18.

```
<!-- #include file="adovbs.inc" -->
<%
    set conn = Server.CreateObject("ADODB.Connection")
    conn.open "DRIVER=Client Access ODBC Driver (32-bit); " & _
              "UID=user; PWD=secret; System=192.168.0.1;"
    set rst = Server.CreateObject("ADODB.Recordset")

    Dim Cart, numLines
    redim Cart(4,999)
    'Read in session variables
    Cart = Session("Cart")
    numLines = Session("numLines")
    custnum = Session("custnum")

    ' If no order lines, display error.
    If numLines = 0 then
        Response.Redirect "error.asp?msg=" & _
        Server.URLEncode ("No order lines or your session has " & _
        "expired, or you tried to re-submit the form.")
    end if
```

Figure 5.18: This page takes care of writing the order data out to the iSeries (part 1 of 3).

```
'Determine "Next Up" order number
rst.Open "SELECT MAX(ORDNO) FROM ASPORDERS.ORDERHDR",conn
If rst.EOF Then
    oid=1
Else
    If ISNULL(rst.Fields(0)) Then
        oid=1
    Else
        oid=CINT(rst.Fields(0))+1
    End If
End If
rst.Close
Set rst=nothing
ordtotl = 0
For i = 1 To numLines
    ' write order lines to ORDERDTL
    dtlSQL = "INSERT INTO   ASPORDERS.ORDERDTL(ORDNM, " & _
             "ORDLN,ORITEM,ORQTY,ORPRIC) VALUES("
    dtlSQL = dtlSQL & oid
    dtlSQL = dtlSQL & "," & i
    dtlSQL = dtlSQL & ",'" & Cart(1,i)
    dtlSQL = dtlSQL & "'," & Cart(3,i)
    dtlSQL = dtlSQL & "," & Cart(4,i)
    dtlSQL = dtlSQL & ")"
    conn.execute dtlSQL
    'Calculate total order value
    ordtotl = ordtotl + (Cart(3,i) * Cart(4,i))
    ' Update in stock in ITEMMAST
    invupSQL= "UPDATE ASPORDERS.ITEMMAST SET ITINST=ITINST-" & _
    Cart(3,i)
    invupSQL = invupSQL & " WHERE ITEMNO='" & Cart(1,i) & "'"
    conn.execute invupSQL
Next
'Write out order header
hdrSQL = "INSERT INTO ASPORDERS.ORDERHDR(ORDNO, ORCUSN, ORTOTL)"
hdrSQL = hdrSQL & " VALUES(" & oid & "," & custnum & "," & _
ordtotl & ")"
conn.execute hdrSQL
errstr=""
'Generate Order Printout from RPG
conn.execute "CALL ASPORDERS.ORD001RP(" & right("0000000000" & _
oid,10) & ".00000)"
If conn.Errors.Count > 0 then
    For e=0 to conn.Errors.Count-1
        errstr = errstr & conn.Errors(e).Description
    Next
```

Figure 5.18: This page takes care of writing the order data out to the iSeries (part 2 of 3).

```
    conn.Close
    Response.Redirect "error.asp?msg=" & _
    Server.URLEncode ("Not succeeded. Error: ") & errstr
    Else
        conn.Close
        Response.Redirect "thanks.asp"
    End If
%>
```

Figure 5.18: This page takes care of writing the order data out to the iSeries (part 3 of 3).

This page writes out header and detail lines using the SQL "INSERT INTO" statement. The data for each of the detail lines is read from the array stored in the Session variable named "Cart." This page also uses an SQL "UPDATE" statement to recalculate the in-stock quantities in ITEMMAST by deducting the order quantity.

After the order data is written out and all updates are complete, an ADO Command object calls the RPG program ORD001RP mentioned at the beginning of this chapter. This program generates a printout of the order data. After that, the Session variables are cleared using the Session.Abandon method. Finally, the page Thanks.html is displayed, showing a message thanking the customer for the order and giving him or her the opportunity to return to the catalog.

Summary

This example of a basic order-entry/shopping-cart system gives you a good idea of what it takes to create an application using ASP. As you can see, it's relatively easy to do. Within the scripts that make up this example, ADO is used to read, write, and update data to the iSeries data source. Since the database access is based on SQL statements, it's easy to take one application and copy it, with a little modification, to access a different file.

Chapter 6 explores another application that performs data access using ASP. In that chapter, you'll see how to create an ad hoc reporting tool that dynamically builds its reports using data on the iSeries.

6

Ad Hoc Sales Reporting with ASP

If your company is like most, a large portion of your time is probably devoted to writing sales reports on the iSeries. What if you could add all of that time back into your schedule? In this chapter, you'll learn how to create an ASP application that allows users to create ad hoc sales reports in a Web browser. You'll even see how to add things like charts and graphs to the report.

First, the Data

Chapter 4 showed a simple example of reading iSeries data and writing it out to the browser as a report. However, unlike a printed page, a Web browser is made to be interactive. This gives you the ability to create reports that are intuitive, allowing the user to re-sort or change the view of data on the fly. You will learn how to do this for a sales report in this chapter.

The sales-reporting example uses the three files shown in Table 6.1. The source for these files is in the companion code to this book. These files are pretty self-explanatory. The CUSTOMER and ITEMS files store customer and item information to be used for filtering and grouping, and the SALESDATA file stores the actual, historical sales information.

Table 6.1: Files Used by the Sales-Reporting Application

File Name	Description
SALESDATA	This file contains historical sales data by customer and item, in monthly buckets.
CUSTOMERS	This file contains customer name and address information, in addition to other header-level customer information.
ITEMS	This file contains item descriptions.

The ITEMS file contains a product-group field (PRDGRP), a subgroup field (SUBGRP), and a color field (COLOR). These values will be used to create a hierarchy of item information, where PRDGRP is the highest level and COLOR is the lowest. The CUSTOMER file contains a region field (REGION). This value will be used as the top of a hierarchy that also contains the customer state and name. The SALESDATA file contains a summary by customer and item, broken down by month. When these files are combined, they allow you to generate sales information at several different levels of detail. To build these files, use the CRTPF command shown here:

```
CRTPF FILE(ASPORDERS/filename) SRCFILE(ASPORDERS/QDDSSRC)
```

For the purposes of the application in this chapter, you'll use the same ASPORDERS library as in chapter 5. On your system, you might want to create a separate library, or even use existing files in place of the sample files. To do this, you would obviously have to modify the SQL "SELECT" statements used by the ADO Recordsets in the example. Once these files are in place, you're ready to look at the first part of the application.

Report Definition

The first page in the sales-reporting application allows a user to define the data that should appear within the sales report. The VBScript in this page creates an HTML form that contains three sections. These sections allow the user to first define record selections, then define the type of report to be created, and finally define report fields. Since the source for this page is a little long, I've broken it up into three segments, so you can examine how each piece works.

Selecting Records, Report Type, and Fields

The first portion of the source is shown in Figure 6.1. Notice that ADO
Connection and Recordset objects are declared within the first section of server-
script code, which is surrounded by the <% and %> identifiers. These objects
continue to be used throughout the page. You can do this even though the
VBScript code is mixed with the HTML tags.

```
<HTML><HEAD><TITLE>Sales Reporting</TITLE></HEAD>
<BODY bgcolor="darkred">
<H1 align="center" style="COLOR: white; FONT-FAMILY: sans-serif">
<i>Sales Report Selection</i></H1>
<form name="reportdef" action="salesreport2.asp" method=GET>
<TABLE width="90%">
<tr><th bgcolor="lightgrey" colspan="4" align="left">
<FONT face="sans-serif" color="darkred" size="-2">
Record Selection:</FONT></th></tr>
<TR><TD valign="top">
<FONT face="sans-serif" color="white" size="-2">
Product Group:</FONT></TD>
<TD><SELECT style="WIDTH: 219px" name="PRDGRP" onchange="reload();">
<option selected></option>
<%
PRDGRP=Request.QueryString("PRDGRP")
If PRDGRP="" Then PRDGRP=Session("PRDGRP")

Session("PRDGRP")=PRDGRP
Set conn=Server.CreateObject("ADODB.Connection")
Set rst=Server.CreateObject("ADODB.Recordset")

conn.open "DRIVER=Client Access ODBC Driver (32-bit); " & _
          "UID=user; PWD=secret; System=192.168.0.2;"

rst.Open "SELECT DISTINCT PRDGRP FROM ASPORDERS.ITEMS", conn

Do Until rst.EOF
Response.Write "<option value='" & rst.Fields(0) & "' "
If PRDGRP=Trim(rst.Fields(0)) Then Response.Write "SELECTED"
Response.Write  ">" & rst.Fields(0) & "</option>"
rst.MoveNext
Loop

rst.Close
%>
```

Figure 6.1: This portion of the page dynamically builds an HTML form (part 1 of 4).

```
</SELECT></TD><TD valign="top">
<FONT face="sans-serif" color="white" size="-2">Color:</FONT></TD>
<TD><SELECT style="WIDTH: 219px" name="COLOR">
<option selected></option>
<%
If PRDGRP="" Then
    rst.Open "SELECT DISTINCT COLOR FROM ASPORDERS.ITEMS", conn
Else
    rst.Open "SELECT DISTINCT COLOR FROM ASPORDERS.ITEMS" & _
    " WHERE PRDGRP='" & PRDGRP & "'", conn
End If

Do Until rst.EOF
Response.Write "<option>" & rst.Fields(0) & "</option>"
rst.MoveNext
Loop


rst.Close
%>
</SELECT></TD></TR><TR><TD valign="top">
<FONT face="sans-serif" color="white" size="-2">
Sales Region:</FONT></TD>
<TD><SELECT style="WIDTH: 219px" name="REGION" onchange="reload();">
<option selected></option>\
<% REGION=Request.QueryString("REGION")
If REGION="" Then REGION=Session("REGION")

Session("REGION")=REGION
rst.Open "SELECT DISTINCT REGION FROM ASPORDERS.CUSTOMERS", conn

Do Until rst.EOF
Response.Write "<option value='" & rst.Fields(0) & "' "
If Request.QueryString("REGION")=Trim(rst.Fields(0)) Then
Response.Write "SELECTED"
Response.Write  ">" & rst.Fields(0) & "</option>"
rst.MoveNext
Loop


rst.Close
%>
</SELECT></TD><TD valign="top">
<FONT face="sans-serif" color="white" size="-2">State:</FONT></TD>
<TD><SELECT style="WIDTH: 219px" name="STATE">
<option selected></option>
```

Figure 6.1: This portion of the page dynamically builds an HTML form (part 2 of 4).

```
<%
If REGION="" Then
    rst.Open "SELECT DISTINCT STATE FROM ASPORDERS.CUSTOMERS", conn
Else
    rst.Open "SELECT DISTINCT STATE FROM ASPORDERS.CUSTOMERS " & _
    " WHERE REGION='" & REGION & "'", conn
End If


Do Until rst.EOF
Response.Write "<option>" & rst.Fields(0) & "</option>"
rst.MoveNext
Loop


rst.Close
%></SELECT></TD></TR><TR><TD valign="top">
<FONT face="sans-serif" color="white" size="-2">
Sales Period:</FONT></TD>
<TD><SELECT style="WIDTH: 219px" name="PERD">
<option selected></option>
<%                              <%
rst.Open "SELECT DISTINCT SAYR, SAPR FROM ASPORDERS.SALESDATA", conn


Do Until rst.EOF
Response.Write "<option value='" & rst.Fields(0) & rst.Fields(1) & "' "
Response.Write ">" & rst.fields(1) & "/" & rst.Fields(0) & "</option>"
rst.MoveNext
Loop


rst.Close
%>
</SELECT></TD></tr><tr><td> </td></tr></TABLE>
<TABLE width="90%">
<tr><th bgcolor="lightgrey" colspan="4" align="left">
<FONT face="sans-serif" color="darkred" size="-2">
Report Type:</FONT></th></tr>
<TR><TD valign="top" width=15%>
<FONT face="sans-serif" color="white" size="-2">
Report Type:</FONT></TD>
<TD><SELECT style="WIDTH: 450px;" name="REPTYPE" size=4>

<option value='1'>Comparative (MTD & YTD Verses Last Year)</option>
<option value='2'>12 Month Trend</option>
<option value='3'>Margin Analysis</option></SELECT></TD></TR><tr>

<td> </td></tr></TABLE>
```

Figure 6.1: This portion of the page dynamically builds an HTML form (part 3 of 4).

```
<TABLE width="90%" ID="Table1"><tr>
<th bgcolor="lightgrey" colspan="4" align="left">
<FONT face="sans-serif" color="darkred" size="-2">
Field Selection:</FONT></th></tr><TR><TD valign="top" width=15%>
<FONT face="sans-serif" color="white" size="-2">Fields:</FONT></TD>
<TD><SELECT style="WIDTH: 450px;" name="FIELDS" size=4 multiple>
<option value='ITEMNO'>Item Number</option>
<option value='ITDESC'>Item Description</option>
<option value='COLOR'>Color</option>
<% if PRDGRP="" Then Response.Write "<option value='PRDGRP'>
Product Group</option>" %>
<option value='CUSTNO'>Customer #</option>
<option value='CNAME'>Customer Name</option>
<option value='STATE'>State</option>
<% if REGION="" Then Response.Write "
<option value='REGION'>REGION</option>" %>
</SELECT></TD></TR><tr><td> </td></tr></TABLE>
<TABLE width="90%">
<tr><td align=right>
<input type=submit value="Next"></td></tr></table></form>
```

Figure 6.1: This portion of the page dynamically builds an HTML form (part 4 of 4).

The code reads in the value of the Querystring variable PRDGRP at the beginning of the source using Request.Querystring("PRDGRP"). If the value is blank, it reads the value of the Session variable of the same name, using Session("PRDGRP"). The value of the variable PRDGRP is then fed back into the Session variable. This is done to ensure that this value is saved throughout the life of the session because this variable relates to one of the list boxes within the form on this page. When one of the values is changed, the other list boxes are adjusted to reflect only values that are valid based on the change. For example, if the Bicycle product group is selected, and the database only has sales data for items in that product group with colors of blue and pink, the COLOR list box will be adjusted accordingly.

The record-selection portion of the form is created by selecting values from the Customer Master and Item Master files, in addition to the date fields from the Sales History files. These values are used to populate several list boxes. The ONCHANGE event is defined on the PRDGRP and REGION list boxes. When this event fires, a client script is run that causes the browser to reload the page while sending in a Querystring variable containing the value of the list box. This value is then used to filter the options available in the COLOR and/or STATE list boxes to show only those options that are valid for the selected PRDGRP or REGION value. Each of the list boxes is populated using the Response.Write method to output HTML <OPTION> elements that contain the field values read from the ADO Recordset through the rst.Fields() property.

The next part of this first form allows a user to select the type of report to be generated. The first option is a MTD/YTD comparative report, containing sales information for a defined period compared to the same period from the prior year, as well as year-to-date comparisons for the same period. The second option is a 12-month trend analysis. This report displays sales data in 12 monthly buckets. The final option is a margin analysis, which compares sales dollars to cost-of-sales dollars for the defined period.

The final part of this form enables the user to define the fields that will appear on the report by selecting them from a list box. The user can select more than one field in the list through the use of the MULTIPLE keyword on the SELECT element. The Next button on the bottom of the form acts as a SUBMIT button, sending these values to the next page.

Running a Saved Report

The second portion of the example page, shown in Figure 6.2, contains a second form that allows the user to select a previously saved report and run it. (You'll learn how reports are saved a little later.) The list of saved reports is built by reading each of the text files in the folder SavedReportURLS, which is a sub-folder of the SalesReport application folder. These files are read in using Scripting.FileSystemObject, which allows the scripts to have access to physical drives, files, and folders on the server.

This example creates a Filesystem object named fldr, using the GetFolder method. This method associates the new Filesystem object with the path specified, in this case the folder "C:\inetpub\wwwroot\SalesReports \SavedReportURLs\." This new object contains the Files collection from which individual files in the folder can be retrieved as items of the collection.

```
<form name="LOAD" action="javascript:openreport();">
<TABLE width="90%" ID="Table2">
   <tr>
      <th bgcolor="lightgrey" colspan="4" align="left">
      <FONT face="sans-serif" color="darkred" size="-2">
      Load Existing Report:</FONT></th>
   </tr>
   <TR>
   <TD valign="top" width=15%>
   <FONT face="sans-serif" color="white" size="-2">
   Report Description:</FONT></TD>
   <TD><SELECT style="WIDTH: 450px;" name="LOADREPORT">

<%  Set fso=Server.CreateObject("Scripting.FileSystemObject")
    const ForReading=1, ForWriting = 2

Set fldr=fso.GetFolder("C:\Inetpub\wwwroot\SalesReporting\
SavedReportURLs")

For each filen in fldr.Files
   set urlfile=fso.OpenTextFile(filen.path,ForReading)
   optionname=urlfile.ReadLine
   optionurl=urlfile.readline
   response.Write "<option value='" & optionurl & "'>" & optionname & _
                  "</option>"
   urlfile.Close
Next %></select></td></tr><tr><td colspan = 2 align=right>

<input type=submit value="Next" ID="Submit1" NAME="Submit1">
</td>
</tr>
</table>
</form>
```

Figure 6.2: This code loads a list of saved reports into an HTML form.

Each item in the collection is read using a For Each. In statement. This allows each file name within the specified folder name to be read. This value is then used with the OpenTextFile method of FileSystemObject to read in each of these files. The first line in these text files contains a descriptive name to be displayed in the list box. The second line contains the Querystring data for the saved report. Each line is read in sequentially, using the ReadLine method. Each of the values read in is then added to the list box, using Response.Write to create an <OPTION></OPTION> element for each report.

Defining Options

The final portion of the code for this page is shown in Figure 6.3. It contains two client-side scripts, both written in JavaScript.

```
<SCRIPT language="javascript">
  function reload() {
  var srcElement = window.event.srcElement;
  window.navigate('salesreport1.asp?' + srcElement.name + '='
  +srcElement.value);
  }
  function openreport() {
  window.navigate('salesreport3.asp?' + LOAD.LOADREPORT.value);
  }
</SCRIPT>
</BODY>
</HTML>
```

Figure 6.3: This client script is the third part of the first page.

The reload() function is used as the ONCHANGE event for the list boxes in the form created in Figure 6.1. The value of the field srcElement.value represents the value selected in the list box that fired the event. This value is used, along with the window.navigate function, to reload this page and supply a simple Querystring variable whose name matches the name of the field within the form. The resulting URL supplied to the function would look something like this:

```
http://Webserver/SalesReporting/salesreport1.asp?PRDGRP=BICYCLE
```

The openreport() client-side JavaScript function is used by the HTML form created in Figure 6.2. This function also uses the window.navigate function, but this time it redirects the user to the third page of the sales-reporting application, and passes the value of the LOADREPORT field. As mentioned earlier, this value will be the full Querystring for the saved report. This will feed all of the Querystring variables used to create the original report into the final page of the application, and cause the report to be generated.

Figure 6.4 shows how Salesreport1.asp will appear in the browser window.

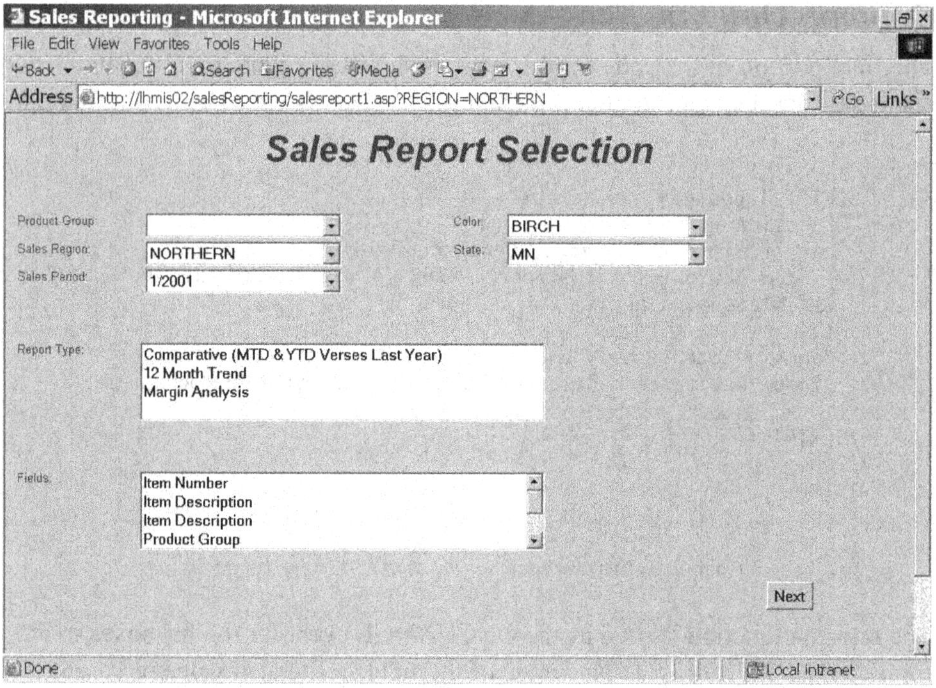

Figure 6.4: This page is used to define options for the report application.

If the Next button on the form in Figure 6.4 is used, the values selected are passed through Querystring variables to the second page of the application, Salesreport2.asp. The source for this page is shown in Figure 6.5.

```
<HTML>
<HEAD><TITLE>Sales Reporting</TITLE></HEAD>
<BODY bgcolor="darkred">
<H1 align="center" style="COLOR: white; FONT-FAMILY: sans-serif">
<i>Sales Report Selection</I></H1>
<form name="reportdef" action="salesreport3.asp" method=GET>
<TABLE width="90%">
<%
Response.Write "<TR bgcolor=lightgrey ><th align='left'>" & _
    "<FONT face='sans-serif' color='darkred' size='-2'>" & _
    "Sorting and Grouping:</FONT></th>"
```

Figure 6.5: This page reads the selected fields, to allow sorting and grouping definitions (part 1 of 3).

```
For x=0 to Request.QueryString("Fields").Count
Response.Write "<TH valign='top'> " & _
"<FONT face='sans-serif' color='darkred' size='-1'>" & x & "</th>"
Next
Response.Write "<th align='center'><FONT face='sans-serif'
color='darkred' size='-2'>Group?</FONT></th>"
Itm=0
For Each fld in Request.QueryString("Fields")
Response.Write "<TR><TD valign='top'><FONT face='sans-serif'
color='white' size='-1'>"
Select Case fld
   Case "PRDGRP"
      Response.Write "Product Group"
   Case "ITEMNO"
      Response.Write "Item Number"
   Case "ITDESC"
      Response.Write "Item Description"
   Case "COLOR"
      Response.Write "Color"
   Case "CUSTNO"
      Response.Write "Customer number"
   Case "CNAME"
      Response.Write "Customer Name"
   Case "REGION"
      Response.Write "Region"
   Case "STATE"
      Response.Write "State"
End Select
Itm=Itm+1
Response.Write "</FONT></TD>"
For x=0 to Request.QueryString("Fields").Count
Response.Write "<td valign='top' align='center'>" & _
   "<input onclick='sortchange(" & x & ");' type=radio name=sort" &_
   & itm & " value=" & x
If x=0 then response.Write " checked "
Response.Write " id=sort" & itm & "></input></td>"
Next
Response.Write "<td align=center><input type=checkbox disabled " & _
               "name=grpsort" & itm &" ID=grpsort" & itm &"></td>"
Response.Write "</tr>"
Next

For Each q in Request.QueryString
For each f  in Request.Que
Response.Write "<input type=hidden name='" & q & "' value=" & f & ">"
Next
Next
```

Figure 6.5: This page reads the selected fields, to allow sorting and grouping definitions (part 2 of 3).

```
%>
</table>
<TABLE width="90%">
<tr><td align=right><input type=submit value="Next"></td></tr>
</table>
</form>

<SCRIPT language="javascript">
function sortchange(val) {
var val;
var srcElement=window.event.srcElement;
var chk=document.all('grp' + srcElement.id);
chk.disabled=false;
if (val == 0) {
chk.disabled=true;
}
}
</SCRIPT>
</BODY>
</HTML>
```

Figure 6.5: *This page reads the selected fields, to allow sorting and grouping definitions (part 3 of 3).*

This page lists the fields to be displayed on the report using the values from the Field Querystring variable, which appeared on the first form in Salesreport1.asp. When multiple values are selected, multiple instances of the Field variable are passed. Each value is accessed in the same way that you would access individual elements within an array, as shown here:

```
FieldValue=Request.QueryString("Fields")(array index)
```

In this example, the array index is a value between zero and one less than the number of values within the collection. To determine how many instances of a given Querystring variable exist, use the Count property, as shown below:

```
Items=Request.QueryString("Fields").Count
```

The description displayed is determined using the Select Case statement, to allow for each possible field name passed. The proper descriptive text is then assigned based on that field name. Along with each field description, a set of radio buttons is displayed to allow the user to define the sort order for the report. The number of radio buttons displayed will match the number of fields selected on the previous page.

There are also check boxes alongside each of the fields. These allow the user to decide whether or not to create subtotal groups on the field. If a field is not to be used for sorting purposes, a value of zero can be specified. The client-side JavaScript function sortchange() disables the grouping check box that corresponds to a field, if the field is not used for sorting.

The document.all JavaScript function gives access to all of the elements in a page where the ID matches the ID specified. In this case, the ID will be Grpsort, followed by a numeric value that represents the field's position on the page. For example, the first line in the field list is 1, and the second is 2. The val variable passed to the JavaScript function will contain a value that represents the radio button selected. If this value is zero, the field has not been selected as a SORT BY field, and cannot be used for grouping. Therefore, the corresponding check box will be disabled.

A sample of the output from the page in Figure 6.5 is shown in Figure 6.6.

Report Generation

When the sorting and grouping have been defined, you're ready to generate the initial report. The information defined on the previous two screens will be used to generate an SQL "SELECT" statement. This statement will be part of the ADO Recordset that will act as the source for the report data.

This is where the application gets a bit more complicated. If there are no grouping levels defined, then the data will simply be displayed in the order defined. Otherwise, you must display subtotals at each of the defined grouping levels. When a group exists, you also need to give the user the ability to hide and show the detail, using a client-side function.

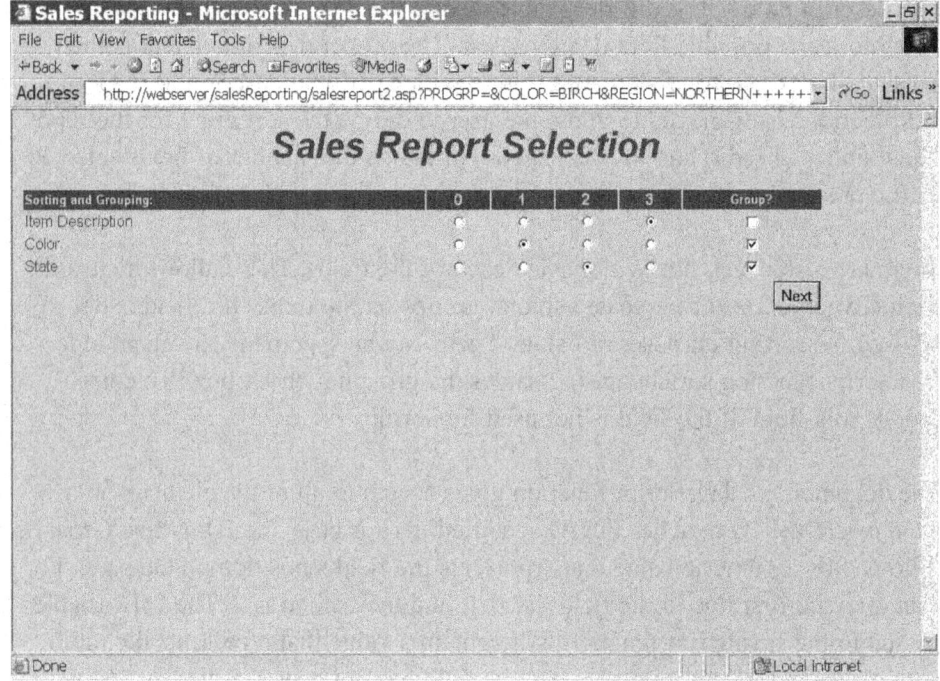

Figure 6.6: This page allows a user to define the sorting and grouping for the report.

Building Page Headings and SQL Source

Again, the source for this page is a little lengthy, so it is divided into chunks, starting with Figure 6.7. The first line of this code uses the <OBJECT> HTML element to incorporate an ActiveX object into the page. In this case, the object is a Microsoft Office Web chart. (You'll see how to use this a little later on.)

The server script begins by defining some of the variables to be used and assigning their values by reading in Querystring variables. Next, it determines the text to be displayed as the report heading, using the Select Case statement along with the Querystring variable Reptype. Within the same Select Case group, it also builds the "SELECT" clause for the SQL statement that will define the ADO Recordset object. This Recordset will be used to access the data for the report.

```
<object id=oChart classid=CLSID:0002E500-0000-0000-C000-000000000046
style='width:320; height:240; position:absolute; top: 0; left:0;
visibility: hidden; color:Coral;' border=4 align=center
VIEWASTEXT></object>
<% 'Definitions
qt = Chr(34)

'ON ERROR RESUME NEXT
'Build data fields for SQL Statement
Yr=Left(Request.QueryString("PERD"),4)
Pr=Right(Request.QueryString("PERD"),2)
If Yr="" Then
    Yr=Year(Now)
    Pr=Month(Now)
End If
grps=0
Level=0
Select Case Request.QueryString("reptype")
'Build Subheading and data selections

    Case 1
    Subhead="Comparative (MTD/YTD vs Last Year)"
    SQLData="SUM(CASE WHEN SAYR=" & Yr & " AND SAPR=" & Pr & _
            "THEN SADLRS ELSE 0 END) AS MTD, " & _
            "SUM(CASE WHEN SAYR=" & Yr & " AND SAPR<=" & Pr & _
            "THEN SADLRS ELSE 0 END) AS YTD, " & _
            "SUM(CASE WHEN SAYR=" & Yr-1 & " AND SAPR=" & Pr & _
            "THEN SADLRS ELSE 0 END) AS MTDLY, " & _
            "SUM(CASE WHEN SAYR=" & Yr-1 & " AND SAPR<=" & Pr & _
            "THEN SADLRS ELSE 0 END) AS YTDLY "

    Case 2
    Subhead="12 Month Trend"
    SQLData=""
    Y=0
    For X=Pr+1 to 12
    Y=Y+1
    SQLData=SQLDataq & " SUM(CASE WHEN SAYR=" & Yr-1 & _
    " AND SAPR=" & X & " THEN SADLRS ELSE 0 END) AS PERD" & Y & ", "
    Next
    For X=1 to Pr
    Y=Y+1
    SQLData=SQLData & "SUM(CASE WHEN SAYR=" & Yr & "AND SAPR=" & X & _
    " THEN SADLRS ELSE 0 END) AS PERD" & Y
    If X<Pr Then SQLData=SQLData & ", "
        Next
```

Figure 6.7: This section of Salesrepor3.asp builds the data source and displays report headers (part 1 of 4).

167

```
     Case 3
     Subhead="Margin Analysis"
     SQLData="SUM(CASE WHEN SAYR=" & Yr & " AND SAPR=" & Pr & _
          "THEN SADLRS ELSE 0 END) AS MTD_$, " & _
          ",SUM(CASE WHEN SAYR=" & Yr & " AND SAPR=" & Pr & _
          "THEN SACOST ELSE 0 END) AS MTD_COST, " & _
          ",SUM(CASE WHEN SAYR=" & Yr & " AND SAPR=" & Pr & _
          "THEN SADLRS-SACOST ELSE 0 END) AS MTD_MARGIN, " & _
          ",SUM(CASE WHEN SAYR=" & Yr & " AND SAPR<=" & Pr & _
          "THEN SADLRS ELSE 0 END) AS YTD_$, " & _
          ",SUM(CASE WHEN SAYR=" & Yr & " AND SAPR<=" & Pr & _
          "THEN SACOST ELSE 0 END) AS YTD_COST, " & _
          ",SUM(CASE WHEN SAYR=" & Yr & " AND SAPR<=" & Pr & _
          "THEN SADLRS-SACOST ELSE 0 END) AS YTD_MARGIN "
End Select
Subh2=""

If Request.QueryString("PERD")<>"" Then Subh2=Subh2 & " Period = " &
    Pr & "/" & Yr
If Request.QueryString("PRDGRP")<>"" Then Subh2=Subh2 &
    " Product Group = " & Request.QueryString("PRDGRP")
If Request.QueryString("STATE")<>"" Then Subh2=Subh2 & "State = " &
Request.QueryString("STATE")
If Request.QueryString("COLOR")<>"" Then Subh2=Subh2 & "Color = " &
Request.QueryString("COLOR")
If Request.QueryString("REGION")<>"" Then Subh2=Subh2 & "Region = " &
Request.QueryString("REGION")

'Build SQL Statement
Redim Sort(Request.QueryString("Fields").Count)
Redim Grp(Request.QueryString("Fields").Count)
SQLFields=" "
SQL=" "
For x=1 to Request.QueryString("Fields").Count
   FieldName=Request.QueryString("Fields")(x)
   SQLFields=SQLFields & FieldName
   If X<Request.QueryString("Fields").Count Then
      SQLFields=SQLFields & ","
   If Request.QueryString("sort" & x)>"0" Then
      Sort(Request.QueryString("sort" & x))=FieldName
   If Request.QueryString("grpsort" & X)="on" Then
      grp(grps)=FieldName
      grps=grps+1
   End If
   End If
Next
```

Figure 6.7: This section of Salesrepor3.asp builds the data source and displays report headers (part 2 of 4).

```
SQLSort=""
SQLGrp=""

For X=1 to Request.QueryString("Fields").Count
    If X>1 Then
    If Sort(x)<>"" Then SQLSort=SQLSort & ","
    End If
    SQLSort=SQLSort & Sort(x)
Next

IF SQLSort<>"" Then
    SQL="SELECT " & SQLSort & ","
Else
    SQL=" SELECT " & SQLFields & ","
End If

If SQLSort<>"" Then
    SQLGrp=" GROUP BY " & SQLSort
    SQLSort=" ORDER BY " & SQLSort
Else
    SQLGrp=" GROUP BY " & SQLFields
End If
SQL = SQL & SQLData
SQL = SQL & " FROM ASPORDERS.SALESDATA INNER JOIN
        ASPORDERS.CUSTOMERS ON SACUSN=CUSTNO " & _
        " INNER JOIN ASPORDERS.ITEMS ON SAITEM=ITEMNO "
SQL = SQL &   SQLGrp
SQL = SQL &   SQLSort

'Create ADO objects
Set conn=Server.CreateObject("ADODB.Connection")
Set rs=Server.CreateObject("ADODB.Recordset")

conn.open "DRIVER=Client Access ODBC Driver (32-bit); " & _
          "UID=user; PWD=secret; System=192.168.0.2;"

rs.Open sql, conn
'Define report grouping arrays
Redim SubTot(rs.Fields.Count-Request.QueryString("Fields").Count, 10)
Redim hldgrp(grps)

'Output headings
Response.Write "<h3 align='center' style='COLOR: white;
FONT-FAMILY: sans-serif'>" & Subhead & "</h3>"
```

Figure 6.7: This section of Salesrepor3.asp builds the data source and displays report headers (part 3 of 4).

169

```
Response.Write "<h4 align='center' style='COLOR: white;
FONT-FAMILY: sans-serif'>" & Subh2 & "</h4>"
%>
<table width=100%><tr>
<td><a class=Heading href="spreadsheet.asp?sql= <% =SQL %>">
View as Spreadsheet</a></td>
<td align=right class=Heading>
<form name=save action='savereport.asp' method=GET>
Report Description:
<% for each fld in Request.QueryString
    Response.Write "<input type=hidden name='" & fld & "' value='" &
    Request.QueryString(fld) & "'>"
    Next%>
<input type=text name=reptdesc style="width:240" ID="Text1">
<input type=submit value="Save Report" ID="Submit1" NAME="Submit1">
</form></td></tr></table>
```

Figure 6.7: This section of Salesrepor3.asp builds the data source and displays report headers (part 4 of 4).

In this "SELECT" statement, the field names are formatted in the same order in which they will appear on the report. This simplifies the application logic because the values from the Recordset can simply be read and displayed, no matter which report format was selected. For example, when the 12-month trend report is selected, the "SELECT" clause for the SQL statement will be created so that the values are summarized into a single column for each of the 12 previous months. The code can simply display the field values it read from the Recordset, without having to do any summarizing at that point.

Next, the code determines if any values were selected on the first screen to filter the data displayed. This information is used to create a subheading on the report that identifies what filters were selected.

The next portion of the code builds the full SQL statement for the ADO Recordset. Two Visual Basic arrays are created to store the field names, for sorting and grouping purposes. The values read from the Querystring variables Sort and Grpsort are used to determine the sort order. The sort values are then used to generate the "ORDER BY" SQL clause.

The grouping options, on the other hand, are not used to generate an SQL "GROUP BY" clause. Instead, these fields will be used to generate report subtotals in a manner similar to that used when generating level breaks in an RPG application. The SQL statement does include a "GROUP BY" clause, but this clause actually contains all of the data fields selected for the report on Salesreport1.asp. This will result in a single line of data for whatever field is the lowest level on the report.

The SQL statement created is then used to build the ADO Recordset that will be the basis of the report. The process of building this SQL statement is, in many ways, the same as you would use in a CL program to dynamically create the source for an Open Query File (OPNQRYF) command.

The final portion of the code segment in Figure 6.7 outputs the page headings to the browser. Along with these page headings, the top of this page will show an HTML table and form that can be used to save the report definition. This is the same definition you saw earlier, which is used by Salesreport1.asp. It contains the contents of the complete Querystring.

The <INPUT> element displayed is used to enter a report description. Each variable in the Querystring collection is also added to this form as a hidden input field. This allows you to pass these values to the page Savereport.asp, which actually handles saving the file. You'll examine this page a little later on, along with Spreadsheet.asp, which is another ASP page referenced in this section of the code.

Generating Report Details

Now that the data source has been created and all of the page headings have been displayed, you're ready to display the report details. This is handled by the next section of Salesreport3.asp, shown in Figure 6.8.

Figure 6.8 starts by writing out the headings for the report columns. The code only displays fields that aren't part of the report grouping. The "grouping" field values will be displayed on the subtotal, not as part of the line details.

```
<%
Response.Write "<table width=100% cellpadding=0 cellspacing=0
border=0 class='Detail'><tr bgcolor=White>"

For x=0 to rs.Fields.count-1
    if ScanArr(rs.Fields(x).Name, grp)=-1 Then
    Response.Write "<th>" & rs.Fields(x).Name & "</th>"
Next

Response.Write "</tr>"
Do until rs.EOF
'Output Detail Lines
Response.Write "<tr bgcolor=LightCoral id='Level" & Level & "det'
style='display:'>"
Y=0

For x=0 to rs.Fields.count-1
    If rs.Fields(x).Type=131 Then
        Response.Write "<td align=right>" & _
            FormatNumber(rs.Fields(x),2) & "</td>"
        For h=0 to grps-1
        SubTot(Y, h) = SubTot(Y,  h) + CDBL(rs.Fields(x).Value)
        Next
        Y=Y+1
    Else
        if ScanArr(rs.Fields(x).Name, grp)=-1 Then
            Response.Write "<td>" & rs.Fields(x) & "</td>"
    End If
Next
Response.Write "</tr>"

For z=0 to grps-1
hldgrp(z)=rs.Fields(grp(z))
Next
rs.MoveNext

'Level Break Control
If Not rs.EOF Then
For z=grps-1 to 0 step -1
If rs.Fields(grp(z))<>hldgrp(z) Then
Response.Write "<tr class='Heading' valign='top'><td colspan=" &
Request.QueryString("Fields").Count-grps-1 & " onclick='showhide()'
style='cursor:hand;' class='Heading' " & _
" id='Level" & level & "' nowrap>" & grp(z) & ": " & hldgrp(z)
```

Figure 6.8: This section of the page generates the sales report (part 1 of 3).

```
response.write "<img align=right style='cursor:hand' src='chart.jpg'
onmouseout='oChart.style.visibility=" & qt & "hidden" & qt & "'
onmouseover='DisplayChart(" & qt & grp(z) & ": " & Trim(hldgrp(z))
& qt & ","
valus=0
For X=0 To 11
   If x<=Y-1 Then
   Response.Write FormatNumber(SubTot(x, z),2,False,False,False) & ", "
   Response.Write qt & rs.Fields(x+(rs.Fields.Count-y)).Name & qt & ","
   valus=valus+1
   Else
      Response.Write "0, " & qt& qt & ","
   End If
Next
Response.Write valus & ")'></td>"
Level=Level+1
For X=0 To Y-1
   Response.Write "<td align=right>" &
   FormatNumber(SubTot(x, z),2) & "</td>"
   SubTot(x, z)=0
Next
End If
Next
Else
For z=grps-1 to 0 step -1
Response.Write "<tr class='Heading' valign='top'><td colspan=" &
Request.QueryString("Fields").Count-grps-1 & " onclick='showhide()'
style='cursor:hand;' class='Heading' " & _
" id='Level" & level & "' nowrap>" & grp(z) & ": " & hldgrp(z)

response.write "<img align=right style='cursor:hand' src='chart.jpg'
onmouseout='oChart.style.visibility=" & qt & "hidden" & qt & "'
onmouseover='DisplayChart(" & qt &  grp(z) & ": " &
            Trim(hldgrp(z)) & qt & ","
valus=0
For X=0 To 11
   If x<=Y-1 Then
   Response.Write FormatNumber(SubTot(x,z),2,False,False,False) & ", "
   Response.Write qt & rs.Fields(x+(rs.Fields.Count-y)).Name & qt & ","
   valus=valus+1
   Else
      Response.Write "0, " & qt& qt & ","
   End If
Next
Response.Write valus & ")'></td>"

Level=Level+1
```

Figure 6.8: This section of the page generates the sales report (part 2 of 3).

```
For X=0 To Y-1
   Response.Write "<td align=right>" & FormatNumber(SubTot(x, z),2) &
   "</td>"
   SubTot(x, z)=0
Next
Next
End If
Loop
```

Figure 6.8: This section of the page generates the sales report (part 3 of 3).

Next, it writes out each detail line by reading through the Recordset and writing out the contents of each of its fields. As mentioned earlier, this is the advantage to building the SQL statement in a way that matches the format of the data to be output. If the field has a type of 131, indicating a numeric value, the value is added to the subtotals. Although an array is being used to store the subtotal values, the general technique is very similar to what you would do in RPG.

At the beginning of the detail line, a bitmap image named Chart.jpg is added. This bitmap displays a chart of the data on each detail or summary line. The image has an ONMOUSEOVER event, which will cause the chart to be displayed, and an ONMOUSEOUT event, which will cause the chart to disappear. (You'll see how this is accomplished later in this chapter.)

If field grouping was defined, the code outputs subtotal lines to define groups of data within the page. The ID property on the group is defined so that it can be matched to the ID property for each of the table rows that make up the detail section. The DISPLAY attribute is used to display or hide the details within each group. A DISPLAY attribute of None causes the rows to be hidden on the screen, while a blank DISPLAY attribute will cause the rows to appear.

The JavaScript function showhide() is called when the user clicks on the subtotal portion. This function will display or hide the details by changing the value of the CLASS property. This function is contained in the source file Jscript.js, shown in Figure 6.9.

```
// Display or hide report details
function showhide() {
var srcElement, detid, det, detln, i;
    srcElement=window.event.srcElement;
    detid=srcElement.id + 'det';
    det=document.all(detid);
if (det.length>1) {
for(i = 0; i < det.length; i++){
if (det(i).style.display == 'none'){
    det(i).style.display ='';}
else {
    det(i).style.display ='none';}
}
}
else {
if (det.style.display == 'none'){
    det.style.display ='';}
else {
    det.style.display ='none';}
}
}
// Determine Mouse Position
function MousePos(xy) {
    if (xy == "X") {return event.clientX + document.body.scrollLeft;}
    if (xy == "Y") {return event.clientY + document.body.scrollTop;}
}
```

Figure 6.9: These Javascript functions display data as summary or detail.

The MousePos function in Figure 6.9 will return the current position
of the mouse cursor on the screen. It is used by the client-side VBScript
function that displays the chart. (You'll examine this function later.) The
output from the sales report is shown in Figure 6.10. The top of the page
includes a "Save Report" button. This button saves the current report-selection
data for use at a later time, through the "Load Report" option on
Salesreport1.asp.

When "Save Report" is clicked, the page Savereport.asp is loaded. The source
for this page is shown in Figure 6.11.

When this page initially loads, it checks to see if the form variable Reptname
has a value. If not, control is redirected back to Salesreport3.asp to allow the

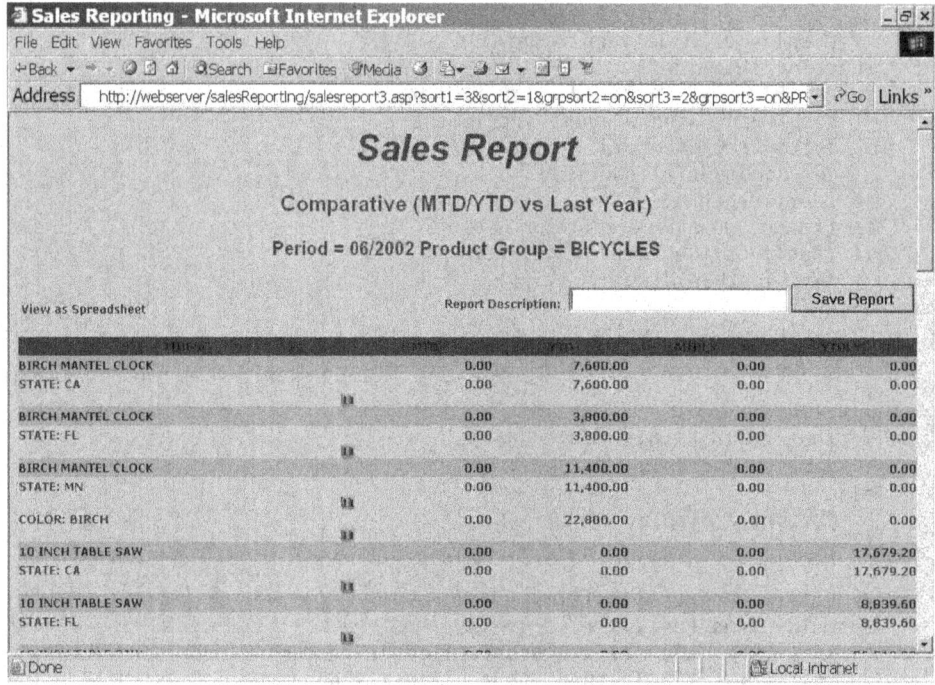

Figure 6.10: This is the finished sales report.

user to enter the description. When Reptname has a value, the Scripting.FileSystemObject component is used to save the report settings to a file. FileSystemObject is used in the way described earlier in this chapter, but this time for writing out to the file using the WriteLine method. The first line writes out the report description, and the second contains the full Querystring used to generate this report.

The information added to this file will be displayed when Salesreport1.asp reads the saved report files in. When the user selects the desired report from the list, the Querystring values are used to redirect control from Salesreport1.asp directly to Salesreport3.asp, while supplying all of the Querystring values required to regenerate the report.

The ability to selectively show and hide the detail section of the data makes this application truly interactive. Now, let's take this one step further by examining some other enhancements.

```
<% const ForReading=1, ForWriting = 2

If Request.Querystring("reptdesc")="" Then
    Response.Redirect("salesreport3.asp?" & Request.Querystring)
End If

Set fso=Server.CreateObject("Scripting.FileSystemObject")

Set fldr=fso.GetFolder("C:\Inetpub\wwwroot\SalesReporting\
SavedReportURLs")

fname=fldr.path & "\Rpt" & year(Now()) & month(now()) & day(now()) & _
      hour(Now()) & Minute(now())& Second(Now()) & ".txt"
set urlfile=fso.OpenTextFile(fname,ForWriting, True)
urlfile.WriteLine Request.Querystring("reptdesc")
urlfile.WriteLine Request.QueryString

urlfile.Close

%>
<SCRIPT language=Javascript>
window.alert("File Saved")
window.history.back(1)
</SCRIPT>
```

Figure 6.11: This ASP script saves the current report settings.

Using the Office Web Components

Once you make an application like this available to users, you might find that they want the ability to manipulate data in different ways. To accommodate this, the sample application includes the ability to display the report data in a Microsoft Excel spreadsheet or chart. To perform this function, either Microsoft Office or the *Office Web Components* (*OWC*) must be installed on the client computer. The setup program for OWC can be found on the Microsoft Office setup CD.

The OWC gives you the ability to display and use Office documents within a browser window. These objects are added to the page using the <OBJECT> HTML tag. In Figure 6.7, the <OBJECT> tag is defined with an ID of oChart and a STYLE of Visibility:Hidden. This prevents the item from being visible on the screen. This chart object also contains the Absolute keyword within the

STYLE definition, indicating that this item is to be positioned using the defined absolute Left and Top positions instead of in the standard flow of the document.

Each of the subtotal groups contains a small icon of a chart. The ONMOUSEOVER event for this image will call the DisplayChart function, which makes the oChart object visible by changing the value of the Visibility parameter. This function also formats the chart values to match the values from the detail section of the report. These values are passed directly into the function through the use of parameters. This is another example of mixing server-side and client-side scripting to achieve the desired results. Before the function displays the chart, it first positions it to match the current mouse position within the page. The source for this function is shown in Figure 6.12.

This function, named DisplayChart, displays a graph when the user places the mouse over the chart image displayed on the subtotal line, firing the ONMOUSEOVER event for the image. This event passes the chart values and headings into the DisplayChart function. This function requires that a chart type of "line" or "bar" be specified, along with 12 chart values and corresponding headings.

The script first determines the number values that should be charted, based on the type of chart defined. The line chart is only used by the 12-month rolling sales report; the other two reports use a bar chart. Next, it positions the chart object named oChart at the current mouse location, using the MousePos function shown in Figure 6.9. Then, it deletes any existing chart data to ensure a clean slate.

The chart is built up using the oChart.Charts.Add(0) statement. In this statement, oChart represents the object, Charts represents the object's Charts collection, and the Add(0) method instructs the control to add a new chart numbered zero. The field values and headings are fed into the chart object by first moving them into a Visual Basic array. Next, the chart type is defined, using the constant chChartTypeColumnClustered for a bar chart or chChartTypeArea for a line chart. Then, the required chart series are added to the chart, and the values and headings are moved in using the SetData method on the chart series. This function requires three parameters.

```
'Show OWC Chart
Function DisplayChart(ChtHdg, Val1, Hdg1, Val2, Hdg2, Val3, Hdg3,
Val4, Hdg4,  Val5, Hdg5, Val6, Hdg6, Val7, Hdg7,Val8, Hdg8, Val9,
Hdg9, Val10, Hdg10,Val11, Hdg11, Val12, Hdg1)


If valus<12 Then
   ChtTp="BAR"
Else
   ChtTp="LINE"
End If
   Set oConstant = oChart.Constants
   oChart.style.visibility="Visible"
   oChart.style.Left=MousePos("X")+10
   oChart.style.Top=MousePos("Y")-120

   if oChart.Charts.Count > 0 then oChart.Charts.Delete(0)
   oChart.Charts.Add(0)
   if ChtTp="BAR" Then


      redim vl1(valus/2),vl2(valus/2)
      redim hd1(valus/2),hd2(valus/2)
   For I=0 to (valus/2)-1
      Select Case I
         Case 0
         vl1(I)=Val1
         vl2(I)=Val2
         hd1(I)=hdg1
         hd2(I)=hdg2
         Case 1
         vl1(I)=Val3
         vl2(I)=Val4
         hd1(I)=hdg3
         hd2(I)=hdg4
         Case 2
         vl1(I)=Val3
         vl2(I)=Val4
         hd1(I)=hdg3
         hd2(I)=hdg4
      end select
   Next
oChart.Charts(0).Type=oConstant.chChartTypeColumnClustered
oChart.Charts(0).SeriesCollection.Add 0
oChart.Charts(0).SeriesCollection(0).Scalings(oConstant.chDimValues).
Minimum=0
oChart.Charts(0).SeriesCollection(0).Caption=Grp1
```

Figure 6.12: This VBScript function displays a graph on the page (part 1 of 3).

179

```
oChart.Charts(0).SeriesCollection(0).SetData oConstant.chDimCategories,_
   oConstant.chDataLiteral, hd1
oChart.Charts(0).SeriesCollection(0).SetData oConstant.chDimValues, _
   oConstant.chDataLiteral, vl1
oChart.Charts(0).SeriesCollection.Add 1
oChart.Charts(0).SeriesCollection(1).Scalings(oConstant.chDimValues).
Minimum=0
oChart.Charts(0).SeriesCollection(1).Caption=Grp2
oChart.Charts(0).SeriesCollection(1).SetData oConstant.chDimCategories,_
   oConstant.chDataLiteral, hd2
oChart.Charts(0).SeriesCollection(1).SetData oConstant.chDimValues, _
   oConstant.chDataLiteral, vl2
oChart.Charts(0).HasTitle=-1
oChart.Charts(0).HasLegend=True
oChart.Charts(0).Title.Caption=ChtHdg
end if

if ChtTp="LINE" Then
   redim vls(valus)
   redim hds(valus)
   For I=0 to valus-1
      Select Case I
         Case 0
            vls(I)=Val1
            hds(I)=Hdg1
         Case 1
            vls(I)=Val2
            hds(I)=Hdg2
         Case 2
            vls(I)=Val3
            hds(I)=Hdg3
         Case 3
            vls(I)=Val4
            hds(I)=Hdg4
         Case 4
            vls(I)=Val5
            hds(I)=Hdg5
         Case 5
            vls(I)=Val6
            hds(I)=Hdg6
         Case 6
            vls(I)=Val7
            hds(I)=Hdg7
         Case 7
            vls(I)=Val8
            hds(I)=Hdg8
```

Figure 6.12: This VBScript function displays a graph on the page (part 2 of 3).

```
        Case 8
        vls(I)=Val9
        hds(I)=Hdg9
        Case 9
        vls(I)=Val10
        hds(I)=Hdg10
        Case 10
        vls(I)=Val11
        hds(I)=Hdg11
        Case 11
        vls(I)=Val12
        hds(I)=Hdg12

     end select
   Next
oChart.Charts(0).Type=oConstant.chChartTypeArea
oChart.Charts(0).SeriesCollection.Add 0
oChart.Charts(0).SeriesCollection(0).Caption=Grp1
oChart.Charts(0).SeriesCollection(0).SetData oConstant.chDimCategories,_
   oConstant.chDataLiteral, hds
oChart.Charts(0).SeriesCollection(0).SetData oConstant.chDimValues, _
   oConstant.chDataLiteral, vls
oChart.Charts(0).HasTitle=-1
oChart.Charts(0).HasLegend=True
oChart.Charts(0).Title.Caption=ChtHdg
end if

end function
```

Figure 6.12: This VBScript function displays a graph on the page (part 3 of 3).

- A constant for the data type being provided: chDimCategories for category headings, and chDimValues for chart values.

- A constant that identifies the type of data being provided. In this case, it is chDataLiteral because the actual data for the chart is being provided, as opposed to a range of cells within a spreadsheet.

- The array containing the values to be used.

After these are defined, the script indicates that a title and legend should be displayed on the chart by using the HasTitle and HasLegend properties, respectively. Finally, the title for the chart is set, using the Title.Caption property. The dynamically displayed chart can be seen in Figure 6.13.

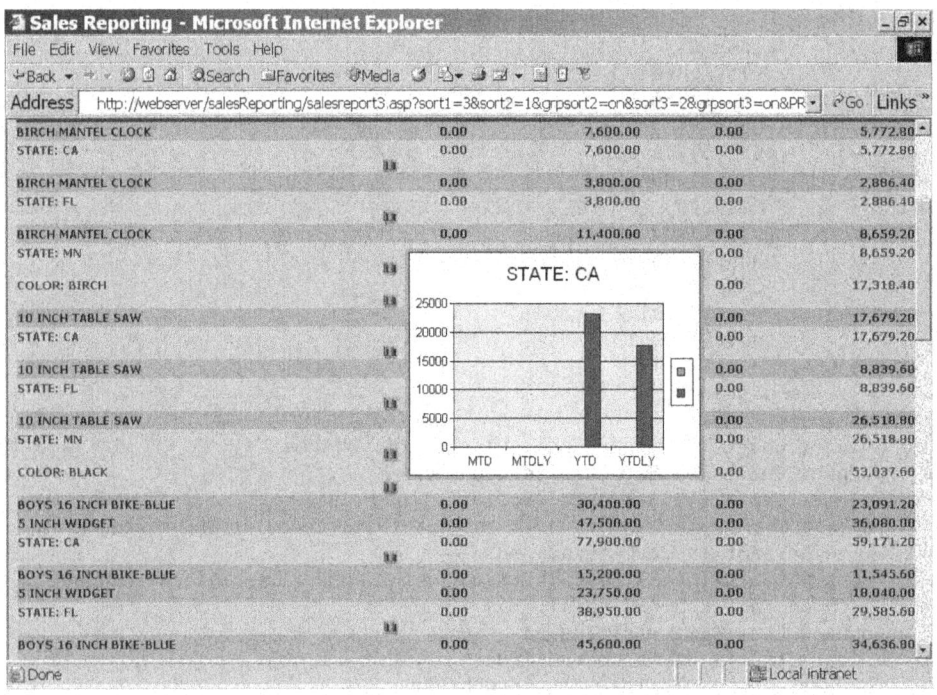

Figure 6.13: The Office Web Chart component is displayed dynamically in the report.

In addition to the Web chart, a hyperlink at the top of the report launches a new window to display the data within the spreadsheet Web component. This is done by passing the SQL string from Salesreport3.asp through a Querystring variable into the page Spreadsheet.asp, which is shown in Figure 6.14.

This page uses the SQL statement generated in Salesreport3.asp to create a new ADO Recordset. The data from this Recordset is fed into the OWC spreadsheet object named Spreadsheet1. This is done by dynamically creating a client-side function that fills in the values for the spreadsheet component. Since the Web component is loaded on the client computer, the server-side script doesn't have access to the object. A client script, however, can access it.

Within the client script, the Activesheet.Range collection accesses the individual cells of the spreadsheet's default sheet, in the following format:

```
<HTML>
<HEAD>
<META NAME="GENERATOR" Content="Microsoft Visual Studio 6.0">
<TITLE></TITLE>
</HEAD>
<BODY>
<object id=Spreadsheet1 classid=CLSID:0002E510-0000-0000-C000-
000000000046 style="width:100%;height:480"></object>
<% SQL=Request.QueryString("SQL")

   Set conn=Server.CreateObject("ADODB.Connection")
   Set rs=Server.CreateObject("ADODB.Recordset")

   conn.open "DRIVER=Client Access ODBC Driver (32-bit); " & _
             "UID=mfaust; PWD=chewie; System=90.0.0.3;"

   rs.Open sql, conn
   Row=1

   response.write "<SCRIPT LANGUAGE='VBScript'>" & Chr(13)
   For x=0 to rs.Fields.Count-1
      response.write "Spreadsheet1.ActiveSheet.Range(" & chr(34) & _
      Chr(65+x) & "1:" & Chr(65+x) & "1" & chr(34) & ").Value="& chr(34) &_
      rs.Fields(x).Name & Chr(34) & chr(13)
   Next

   Do Until rs.EOF
   Row=Row+1
   For x=0 to rs.Fields.Count-1
      response.write "Spreadsheet1.ActiveSheet.Range(" & chr(34) & _
      Chr(65+x) & Row & ":" & Chr(65+x) & Row & chr(34) & ").Value=" & _
      Chr(34) & rs.Fields(x).Value & Chr(34) & chr(13)
   Next
   rs.MoveNext
   Loop
response.write "</SCRIPT>"
%>
</BODY>
</HTML>
```

Figure 6.14: This source generates a page that displays an Office Web spreadsheet.

Range*(upper_left_cell: lower_right_cell)*

The Value property sets the value of these cells. This can either be a constant or a standard formula, such as *=SUM(A1:A3)*. In addition to the Value property,

183

Table 6.2: Properties for Manipulating an OWC Spreadsheet

Property	Description
Font.Size	Sets the font size for the current cell or cell range, in points.
Font.Bold	Defines whether or not to set bold on, using a Boolean (True/False) value.
Halignment	Sets the horizontal alignment for a cell or range, where 0=Automatic, 1=Left, 2=Center, and 3=Right.
Valignment	Sets the vertical alignment for a cell or range, where 0=Top, 1=Middle, and 2=Bottom.
Borders.Weight	Defines the border width of the specified cell or range.
Borders.Color	Defines the color of the border for the specified cell or range.

several other properties are available that can change the appearance of the cells in the spreadsheet. These properties and their descriptions are listed in Table 6.2.

Spreadsheet.asp adds the script statements to populate the spreadsheet object using Response.Write. These additional properties would be written to the browser the same way. These objects can also be used server-side; however, the control itself is used somewhat differently. In the case of the Chart control, the chart is converted to a GIF file so that it can be displayed in the browser. The Spreadsheet object is ported into an HTML table. As you can imagine, in both these cases, the resulting object is much less interactive than the client-side version. It's important to note, however, that since these objects are COM-based, they are not natively compliant with Netscape Navigator or Mozilla. If your application might be used in either of these browsers, you would probably want to design it to use these components server-side.

Summary

The sales-reporting application in this chapter helps illustrate how ASP can be used for more than just external Web applications. This application could easily replace existing RPG (or even Visual Basic) reporting programs. As you've seen, the time to develop this type of application is much less than either of these alternatives, even including nice "extras" as charting and spreadsheet functionality. Some of the scripts used here, like the DisplayChart script, can easily be used in other Web pages you might design in the future.

The next chapter introduces you to ASP.NET and examines what it takes to move applications from ASP to ASP.NET.

7

Moving to ASP.NET

As it so often does, Microsoft has changed the world again, at least when it comes to programming on the Windows platform. Microsoft's *.NET* ("dotnet") framework is the backbone of its vision for Windows application development. The .NET framework offers a *common language runtime (CLR)*, allowing the programmer to develop in any language that is compliant with .NET. The CLR used by .NET handles the loading and executing of code, in addition to exception-handling.

ASP.NET is an extension of the .NET framework, which can be used to add .NET functionality to your Web applications. To add ASP.NET support, you need to install the .NET framework on your Web server. This is available for download from Microsoft's Web site. It is also included with Visual Studio.NET.

Why Go .NET?

Now that you've learned ASP, you might be wondering why you should consider moving to something new, namely ASP.NET. One of the primary reasons is language support. In ASP, you have basically two choices, JavaScript or VBScript. With ASP.NET, the choices get a little broader. In fact, any language that is compliant with the CLR is an available option in ASP.NET. In addition to JavaScript, this list currently includes C# and Visual Basic.NET, which replaces the VBScript language.

Many third-party languages can also be integrated into .NET and therefore become available to the ASP.NET programmer. ASNA, well-known for its Visual RPG product, is planning to release a .NET-compliant implementation of RPG. This would give you the ability to develop ASP.NET Web applications using a language that you're already familiar with.

Changes in ASP.NET

Moving from ASP to ASP.NET is no small task. The good news is that your Web server will support both ASP and ASP.NET applications. This means that you can slowly make the move to ASP.NET, one page at a time. This is possible, in part, because ASP.NET files use the file extension *.aspx* instead of *.asp*, so new and old versions of the same page can coexist in the same folder.

Coding Changes

While you do have access to more languages in ASP.NET, you are limited to one language per page. This limitation doesn't exist with ASP. The language of choice for your page must now be defined within the @PAGE directive, as shown below:

```
<%@PAGE LANGUAGE="Visual Basic"%>
```

The @PAGE directive defines other page-level attributes, as well. A partial list of these attributes is given in Table 7.1.

ASP.NET includes some other important changes related to the Querystring and Form collections. These objects have been changed to NameValueCollections. In most cases, these changes are invisible. However, a slight coding change is

Table 7.1: Attributes That Can Be Defined on the @PAGE Directive

Attribute	Values	Description
ASPCompat	True/False	When set to True, allows use of ASP objects (COM controls). The default value is False.
Buffer	True/False	Defines whether or not data sent to the browser is buffered.
CodeBehind	File name	Identifies the file containing the program code for this page. This can be used to separate the HTML portion of your page from the code portion.
CodePage	Code-page ID	Defines the code page used by the page.
Description	String value	Provides a text description for the page.
ErrorPage	Web page URL	Identifies the page to be displayed if an unhandled error occurs within your page.
Explicit	True/False	Defines whether or not all variables must be defined prior to use. The default value is True.
Transaction	True/False	Defines whether or not transaction processing should be used for this page. This can be compared to commitment control on the iSeries.

required if you need to retrieve multiple values with the same name, as with the Field and Sort Querystring variables in chapter 6. ASP would read these values using the following code:

```
<% Response.Write Request.QueryString("Fields")(0)%>
```

In ASP.NET, the GetValues method would be used to retrieve the values, as shown here:

```
<% Response.Write(Request.QueryString.GetValues("Fields")(1))%>
```

If you are retrieving a variable that contains only one value, the standard method is still acceptable. The same would be true for the Request.Form NameValueCollection and the Request NameValueCollection. Also notice that the string associated with the Response.Write method is now enclosed in parentheses.

In ASP.NET, all global variable and subroutine definitions must be enclosed within a <SCRIPT> block. In ASP, these items could be defined within an ASP (<% %>) code block. While you can define variables within an ASP code block, these variables will not be available to other functions within the page. This change is important because Option Explicit is the default in ASP.NET, where it was not in ASP. When the Option Explicit keyword is present, all variables must be defined using the Dim statement prior to use. If you're an RPG programmer, this shouldn't be a foreign concept; you're already used to defining your data separately from your code.

For example, the following code would be perfectly acceptable in ASP:

```
<% For X=1 to 24
   Y=PoundstoKilos(x)
   Response.Write x & " Pounds = " & Y & " Kilograms "
   Next X

   Function PoundstoKilos(x)
   Return(x*2.205)
   End Function
%>
```

This would not be supported in ASP.NET. Instead, the variables and subroutines would be defined within a server-side <SCRIPT> block, so the previous example would be converted to the following:

```
<script language="VB" runat="server">
   Dim X
   Dim Y

   Function PoundstoKilos(x As Long) As Long
       Return(x*2.205)
   End Function
</script>
```

```
<% For X=1 to 25
      Y=PoundstoKilos(x)
      Response.Write(x & " Pounds = " & Y & " Kilograms ")
   Next
%>
```

It's important to note the way that, when page data is processed using <SCRIPT> blocks, all code must be defined within a procedure. Therefore, if you want the code to be executed immediately, it must be placed in the Page_Load event, as shown here:

```
<script language="VB" runat="server">
   Sub Page_Load(Source As EventArgs, E As EventArgs)
      Response.Write("Begin Page Here…")
   End Sub
</script>
```

Code placed within <% %> code blocks will be executed top-to-bottom, as the code blocks are encountered at render time. The code within the Page_Load event will be executed prior to any of the other code.

Within VBScript in an ASP, many objects have a default property that is retrieved when the object name is specified by itself. A good example of this is when accessing an item in the Fields collection of a Recordset. In an ASP, the following lines of code would retrieve the value of the field ITEMNO:

```
<% Set conn=Server.CreateObject("ADODB.Connection")
   Set rs= Server.CreateObject("ADODB.Recordset ")

   conn.open "DRIVER=Client Access ODBC Driver (32-bit); " & _
             "UID=user; PWD=secret; System=192.168.0.2;"

   rs.open "SELECT * FROM ITEMMAST", conn

   Do Until rs.EOF
      Response.Write rs.Fields("ITEMNO")
```

```
        rs.MoveNext
    Loop %>
```

In ASP.NET, this code would look somewhat different. For starters, the Fields collection has no default property. The ASP.NET equivalent of this code is as follows:

```
<% conn=Server.CreateObject("ADODB.Connection")
   rs= Server.CreateObject("ADODB.Recordset ")

   conn.open("DRIVER=Client Access ODBC Driver (32-bit); " & _
          "UID=user; PWD=secret; System=192.168.0.2;")

   rs.open("SELECT * FROM ITEMMAST", conn)

   Do Until rs.EOF
      Response.Write(rs.Fields("ITEMNO").value)
      rs.MoveNext
   Loop %>
```

There are some other important changes in this example. As mentioned earlier, all of the values supplied to methods must be specified within parentheses. In addition, the Set statement is no longer used to define an object. Finally, the Value property must be specified to retrieve the field's value.

A major enhancement in ASP.NET is the way that your server-side code interacts with your page elements. In ASP, you really didn't have direct access to any of the HTML elements within the page. This meant that you couldn't read any of the data from your page without passing the data through a Querystring or Form variable.

In ASP.NET, the RUNAT="SERVER" directive can be used with most HTML tags to indicate that the element on which it is defined is available on the server. Not only can the element's value be read or set, but any of its available events can be directed to a server-side procedure. This ability can be extremely valuable when your application needs to verify form data against a database, since the database connectivity is done from the server to the database, and not from the client to the database.

Figure 7.1 shows an example of an ASP.NET form that validates a customer number field from an HTML form against a data source on the iSeries. The first thing you might notice is that the value of the ASPCompat attribute is set to True. This is done so that ADODB objects can be used, since these objects are COM controls. If you don't set ASPCompat to True, you would only have access to .NET controls, not the older COM components. Notice, also, that the server-side script accesses the elements within the HTML portion of the page through their ID attributes.

The example in Figure 7.1 validates the customer number against the file CUS-TOMERS on the iSeries. If the entry is valid, the value of the field CNAME is displayed. If the entry is invalid, an error message is displayed. In either case, the value is displayed by changing the Value property of the <SPAN> element that has an ID of CustName. At the same time, the background color of the HTML table containing the form is changed to red via Table1.BGColor. Notice that the event fired when the SUBMIT button is clicked is not the simple ONCLICK event. Here, the event is ONSERVERCLICK, which identifies that the event is fired on the server, not the client.

The code in Figure 7.1 requires the use the ASPCompat attribute because of ADO. While the ASPCompat attribute does help ease the transition to ASP.NET, there can be a tradeoff in diminished performance. For this example, there is an alternative: *ADO.NET*, which is basically the .NET framework replacement for ActiveX Data Objects.

In ADO, Connection objects are associated with Recordset and/or Command objects. In ADO.NET, Recordsets are replaced by *Datasets*. A Dataset is a mem-ory-resident representation of the desired data. Dataset objects, however, are somewhat more flexible than Recordsets. The tables that make up a Dataset are contained within the DataTableCollection. This collection contains one item for each table in the collection. Each of these tables contains a DataRowCollection, which contains each record within the DataTable, and a DataColumnCollection, which contains the field-level information for each row. The DataTableCollection object also contains data relation information that defines relationships between the DataTable and other tables.

```
<%@PAGE LANGUAGE="VB" ASPCompat="true"%>
<HTML>
<SCRIPT RUNAT="SERVER">
Dim conn As Object

Dim rs As Object

Sub Submit_Proc(sender As Object, e As EventArgs)
   conn=Server.CreateObject("ADODB.Connection")
   rs=Server.CreateObject("ADODB.Recordset ")

   conn.Open("DRIVER=Client Access ODBC Driver (32-bit); " & _
            "UID=user; PWD=secret; System=192.168.0.2;")

   rs.Open("SELECT CNAME FROM ASPORDERS.CUSTOMERS WHERE CUSTNO=" & _
            CUSNO.Value, conn)

   If rs.EOF Then
      CustName.InnerHTML="Invalid Customer"
      Table1.BGColor="RED"
   Else
      CustName.InnerHTML=rs.Fields(0).Value
      Table1.BGColor="WHITE"
   End If
End Sub
</SCRIPT>
<BODY>
<TABLE ID="TABLE1" RUNAT="SERVER" BGCOLOR="WHITE">
<TR><TD>
<FORM NAME="SAMPLE" METHOD="POST" RUNAT="SERVER">
            Customer #:
            <INPUT TYPE="TEXT" ID="CUSNO" SIZE=10 RUNAT="SERVER">
            <INPUT TYPE="SUBMIT" ONSERVERCLICK="Submit_Proc"
               VALUE="Submit" RUNAT="SERVER">
</FORM>
<SPAN ID="CustName" RUNAT="SERVER"></SPAN>
</TD></TR>
</TABLE>
</BODY>
</HTML>
```

Figure 7.1: This example uses server-side access to HTML page elements.

Figure 7.2 modifies the script in Figure 7.1 to read data through ADO.NET. In this version, the first two <%@IMPORT> directives give access to the ADO.NET objects. Also, this script references the IBMDA400 OLE DB provider using the fully qualified name, IBMDA400.DataSource.1.

The Command object in Figure 7.2 is defined in much the same way as it would be defined with ADO. The difference is that you have to use the

```
<%@PAGE LANGUAGE="VB" debug="true"%>
<%@Import Namespace="System.Data"%>
<%@Import Namespace="System.Data.OleDb"%>
<HTML>
<SCRIPT RUNAT="SERVER">
Dim conn As Object

Dim rs As Object

Sub Submit_Proc(sender As Object, e As EventArgs)
   Dim conn As OleDbConnection
   Dim cmd As OleDbDataAdapter
   dim dst As DataSet
   dim tbl As DataTable
   dim i, r As Integer

' Define ADO.NET Connection object
   conn = New OleDbConnection("Provider=IBMDA400.DataSource.1;" & _
          "User ID=user;PASSWORD=secret;Data Source=192.168.0.2;")

' Use ADO.NET Command object to select records
   cmd=New OleDbDataAdapter("SELECT CNAME FROM ASPORDERS. CUSTOMERS" & _
                             "WHERE CUSTNO=" & CUSNO.Value, conn)

' Fill our dataset with the selected data
   dst = New DataSet
   cmd.Fill(dst)

' Define a DataTable for our dataset
   tbl = New DataTable
   tbl = dst.Tables(0)

   If tbl.Rows.Count=0 Then
      CustName.InnerHTML="Invalid Customer"
      Table1.BGColor="RED"
   Else
      CustName.InnerHTML=tbl.Rows(0).Item("CNAME")
      Table1.BGColor="WHITE"
   End If
End Sub
</SCRIPT>
<BODY>
```

Figure 7.2: In this example, ADO is replaced by ADO.NET (part 1 of 2).

```
<TABLE ID="TABLE1" RUNAT="SERVER" BGCOLOR="WHITE">
<TR><TD>
<FORM NAME="SAMPLE" METHOD="POST" RUNAT="SERVER" ID="Form1">
   Customer #:
   <INPUT TYPE="TEXT" ID="CUSNO" SIZE=10
          RUNAT="SERVER" NAME="CUSNO">
   <INPUT TYPE="SUBMIT" ONSERVERCLICK="Submit_Proc"
          VALUE="Submit" RUNAT="SERVER" ID="Submit1">
</FORM>
<SPAN ID="CustName" RUNAT="SERVER"></SPAN>
</TD></TR>
</TABLE>
</BODY>
</HTML>
```

Figure 7.2: In this example, ADO is replaced by ADO.NET (part 2 of 2).

OleDBDataAdapter class to define it. Once the Command object is defined, its contents are added to the Dataset object using the Fill method. Remember that a Dataset is a memory-resident representation of the actual data in a database, so the Fill method retrieves the data from the database into the Dataset.

One Dataset can contain multiple tables that have relationships to one another. A good example would be an order's header record and detail records. Each table would be fed into the Dataset using the technique just shown. Assuming that the header table was defined first, the header file would be accessed using the Tables collection, as DataSet.Tables(0). The detail records would be accessed through the Tables collection using DataSet.Tables(1). The relationship between the tables is defined using the DataRelation class. The following example shows how this DataRelation would be defined between the order header and detail records:

```
Private Sub HdrDtlRelation()

' Use the DataColumn with each of our DataTable objects in the DataSet.
   Dim hdrCol As DataColumn
   Dim dtlCol As DataColumn

' Define the columns to be used within our relation
   hdrCol = dst.Tables("ORDERHDR").Columns("ORDNM")
```

```
    dtlCol = dst.Tables("ORDERDTL").Columns("ORDNO")

' Build the DataRelation object
    Dim As DataRelation
    drlHdrDtl = New DataRelation("HeaderDetail", hdrCol, dtlCol)

' Insert the new DataRelation into the DataSet
    dst.Relations.Add(drlHdrDtl)

End Sub
```

In this example, two DataColumn objects define the related fields between the two tables. Next, the DataRelation object is built and added to the existing Dataset. When you access a record from the header table, the associated detail records are available automatically by using the GetChildRows method on the associated row.

The code shown in Figure 7.3 will read each record from the order header table, and then read the associated records from the order detail table using the GetChildRows method.

```
<%@PAGE LANGUAGE="VB" debug="true"%>
<%@Import Namespace="System.Data"%>
<%@Import Namespace="System.Data.OleDb"%>
<HTML>
<SCRIPT RUNAT="SERVER">
Dim conn As Object
Dim rs As Object

Sub Page_Load(sender As Object, e As EventArgs)
    dim conn As OleDbConnection
    dim cm1 As OleDbDataAdapter
    dim cm2 As OleDbDataAdapter
    dim dst As DataSet
    dim hdr,dtl As DataTable
    dim htmlSrc As String
    dim i, r As Integer
    dim hdrCol As DataColumn
    dim dtlCol As DataColumn
    dim rowarry() As DataRow
```

Figure 7.3: This example uses the DataRelation object to create a hierarchy within a Dataset (part 1of 2).

```
' Define ADO.NET Connection objects
  conn = New OleDbConnection("Provider=IBMDA400.DataSource.1;" & _
        "User ID=user;PASSWORD=secret;Data Source=192.168.0.2;")

' Populate Header DataTable
  cm1 = New OleDbDataAdapter("SELECT * FROM ASPORDERS.ORDERHDR", conn)
  dst = New DataSet
  cm1.Fill(dst, "Hdr")

' Populate the detail DataTable
  cm2 = New OleDbDataAdapter("SELECT * FROM ASPORDERS.ORDERDTL" , conn)
  cm2.Fill(dst, "Dtl")

' Define the columns to be used within our relation
  hdrCol = dst.Tables("Hdr").Columns("ORDNO")
  dtlCol = dst.Tables("Dtl").Columns("ORDNM")
  dst.Relations.Add("HdrDtl", hdrCol, dtlCol,False)

' Define our DataTable objects
  hdr = New DataTable
  hdr = dst.Tables("Hdr")
  dtl = New DataTable
  dtl = dst.Tables("Dtl")
  htmlSrc= ""

  For r=0 to hdr.Rows.Count-1
' Display header data
  htmlSrc=htmlSrc & "Order:" & hdr.Rows(r).Item("ORDNO") & "<br>"
  htmlSrc=htmlSrc & "Customer:" & hdr.Rows(r).Item("ORCUSN") & "<br>"

' Read corresponding detail records using our DataRelation
      rowarry = hdr.Rows(r).GetChildRows("HdrDtl")
      For i=0 to rowarry.GetUpperBound(0)
         htmlSrc=htmlSrc & rowarry(i).Item("ORDLN") & " " & _
         rowarry(i).Item("ORITEM") & " " & _
         rowarry(i).Item("ORQTY") & " " & _
         rowarry(i).Item("ORPRIC") & " " & _
         rowarry(i).Item("ORQTY") * rowarry(i).Item("ORPRIC") & "<br>"
      Next
      htmlSrc = htmlSrc & "<br>"
   Next
OrderData.InnerHTML=htmlSrc
End Sub </SCRIPT>
<BODY><SPAN ID="OrderData" RUNAT="SERVER"></SPAN></BODY>
</HTML>
```

Figure 7.3: This example uses the DataRelation object to create a hierarchy within a Dataset (part 1 of 2).

The parameter supplied to the GetChildRows method in Figure 7.3 matches the name defined on the DataRelation. The resulting rows are moved into the DataRow array named "rowarry." Once the rows are moved into this array, all of the columns from the DataTable are available within the array. They can be accessed through the same method used to access the columns directly from the DataTable:

```
DataTable.Rows(rownum).Item(fieldname)

' or

Array(element=rownum).Item(fieldname)
```

Note that, when you assign the value of the InnerHTML property for a <SPAN> element, you can insert HTML tags into that value. In Figure 7.3, the <BR> tag is used to insert line breaks within the data. As with most .NET features, ADO.NET gives you great added functionality. The tradeoff, as you can see, is its added complexity.

Application-management Changes

In addition to the code changes already mentioned, there are several important changes to the way that you manage your applications within ASP.NET. Possibly the most significant of these is how application configuration settings are stored. With ASP, the settings related to your application, including security, are stored within the system registry, or in the Internet Information Server metabase. To view or maintain these settings, you must use the IIS management console.

In ASP.NET, these settings are kept in an application Web.Config XML file. This makes it much easier to access and change your application configuration, since XML documents are easily readable from your Web browser.

Your application's security settings are one of the items managed by Web.Config. Another is the type of user authentication, which is defined using the "authentication" element. The following four authentication types are available:

- Windows (the default type)

- Form (using a Cookie object)

- Passport (using a Microsoft Passport Account)

- None (No authentication required)

The authentication method is chosen within the Web.Config file as shown here:

```
<system.web>
    <authentication mode="Windows" />
</system.web>
```

This example would set the Windows authentication method, which uses Windows user accounts to validate users. This method is ideal when creating applications that are intended for use on a LAN. However, it's not necessarily the best choice for a more public Web site, since it requires you to manage Windows user accounts.

The Form authentication method allows you to use a custom ASP.NET page and form to authenticate users. The following example shows how this method would be defined in Web.Config:

```
<system.web>
    <authentication mode="Form" />
    <forms forms="LoginFrm" loginUrl="/userlogin.aspx" />
</system.web>
```

Using this type of authentication, a login form is displayed to allow the user to enter credentials. This information is then stored in a Cookie object to allow other pages within the application to have access to these credentials. The downside to this is that your application must control the authentication. This is not necessary using Windows authentication.

The Passport authentication method uses Microsoft's Passport service to authenticate users. This service allows a user to have a single login to get to multiple sites. To use this method, you must register with the Passport service. It provides each site with its own unique key that is used to encrypt data sent between the site to the Passport login server at the time of user authentication. This method also requires the use of the Passport SDK, which can be downloaded from the Passport Web site at *www.passport.com*. While the Passport method is convenient for user authentication, having a server outside of your control perform the authentication might make it slightly less attractive.

The final authentication method is None. As the name suggests, this method can be used if no authentication is required, or if you want to write custom authentication into your ASP.NET application.

To define whether or not specific users have access to the application, the <ALLOW> and <DENY> elements would be specified. These elements are contained within the <AUTHENTICATION> element, as shown here:

```
<system.web>
    <authentication mode="Windows" />
    <allow users="DOMAIN/jsmith" />
    <allow users="DOMAIN2/bjoines" />
    <deny users="*" />
</system.web>
```

This example would deny access to everyone but the two users defined on the <ALLOW> elements. This method of controlling security is somewhat more flexible than that currently available with an ASP.

It's important to note that many of the settings contained in the Web.Config will also appear in the IIS management console. However, the IIS settings are ignored by ASP.NET applications in favor of Web.Config. Some of these settings, security settings for example, work in conjunction with those in the IIS management console. For example, when using Form or Passport authentication, the IIS security setting would need to be set to allow anonymous logins. This would allow the security definition to defer to Web.Config.

Preparing for ASP.NET

You might be wondering why I devoted most of this book to examining ASP, only to change the focus at the end. The answer is pretty simple: ASP is already a very popular platform for developing browser-based applications. ASP.NET, however, is destined to eventually replace ASP. With this in mind, there are things you can do while developing your ASP applications to prepare yourself for ASP.NET.

As you've already discovered, in ASP.NET, you can't define variables or functions within a code block (<% %>). The good news is that these items can be placed in the <SCRIPT> block in both ASP and ASP.NET. For this reason, it's probably a good idea to get in the practice of placing these items in a <SCRIPT> block in your ASP applications.

You also learned that ASP.NET doesn't support multiple server-side scripting languages within a single page. In my opinion, this is a good idea for ASP, too. If you are developing ASP applications, it makes sense to stick to a single language per page, at the very least. Otherwise, it is much more difficult to analyze application flow. For even more continuity, I suggest that you pick a single language to be used by all of the pages that make up your application.

Along this same line, ASP.NET doesn't support the nesting of include files. As you saw in chapter 5, an include file is similar to /COPY. It allows code to be copied into the current page upon execution. *Nested includes*—that, is an include file whose code incorporates another include file—can make it extremely difficult to analyze application flow. When developing ASP applications, I suggest that you avoid using nested includes whenever possible.

Another feature not supported by ASP.NET is *render* subroutines. These subroutines are actually code blocks intermixed with HTML tags, as shown here:

```
<% Sub DisplayTable() %>
<TABLE>
<TR><TD>Cell A</TD><TD>Cell B</TD></TR>
```

```
<TR><TD>Cell C</TD><TD>Cell D</TD></TR>
</TABLE>
<% End Sub %>
<P> Page heading <BR>
<% Call DisplayTags() %>
```

In this example, when the DisplayTable subroutine is called, the table contained between the two code blocks is displayed. Since ASP.NET requires functions and subroutines to be defined within a <SCRIPT> block, render subroutines can't be used. Again, while this ability can be useful in many circumstances, it makes code difficult to analyze and should therefore be avoided, even when developing ASP applications.

Since ASP.NET doesn't support default properties on objects, you should, whenever possible, explicitly define the property being accessed. You saw this with the Value property on the Fields collection of the Recordset object earlier in this chapter. While this can be a bit of a hassle, it's worth it if there's any possibility of moving the application to ASP.NET. Since Option Explicit is the default for ASP.NET, you should get in the habit of explicitly defining all of the variables used by your application.

As you saw with the Response.Write method, ASP.NET requires the use of parentheses around the parameters supplied to a given method. In ASP, this isn't required, but it is supported. Again, if you think that at some point a page might end up in an ASP.NET application, it's probably a good idea to consider using parentheses around the parameters for methods.

Another point to consider in planning for ASP.NET is whether to move your data access applications from ADO to ADO.NET. Remember that the ASPCompat="True" directive will give you the ability to continue to use ADO within an ASP.NET page. On the other hand, the added functionality available with ADO.NET can make moving your applications to ADO.NET an attractive option.

Summary

In the end, deciding whether to write your applications in ASP or ASP.NET (and whether to go with ADO or ADO.NET) depends on several factors that will be specific to your situation. In any case, it's a good idea to have a handle on ASP prior to attempting the jump to ASP.NET—hence, the purpose of this book.

As you've seen throughout this book, ASP gives developers the ability to rapidly develop robust client/server applications using a Web browser as the user interface. ASP.NET builds on this already powerful platform by adding more options for security and data access.

Now it's time to put down the book and get your feet wet. You might find yourself putting ASP applications in place sooner than you ever imagined.

Appendix A

HTML Tag Reference

Document-level Tags

<html></html>	Defines the start and end of the HTML document.
<head></head>	Contains header-level information about the document.

Header-level Tag Used with the <HEAD> Tag

<title></title>	Puts the name of the document in the title bar.
<body></body>	Declares the portion of the HTML document that is displayed to the browser.

Optional Attributes Used with the <BODY> Tag

bgcolor=	Defines the background color of the document.
text=	Defines the default text color.
link=	Sets the color to be used for a hyperlink.
vlink=	Identifies the color to be used for a visited hyperlink.
alink=	Sets the color to be used when a hyperlink is clicked.

Text Formatting

<pre></pre>	Identifies a section of preformatted text. Often used to define program code on a Web page.
<hn ></hn >	Defines a heading font style, where *n* is an integer from one to six. A size of one indicates the largest font, and six indicates the smallest.
<b></b>	Defines bold text.
<i></i>	Causes text to be italicized.
<font></font>	Defines font attributes for the text contained within the tags.

Optional Attributes Used with the <FONT> Tag

color=	Defines the font color.
face=	Identifies the font to be used.
size=	Sets the size of the font.

Hyperlinks

<a></a>	Defines hyperlinks within the document

Optional Attributes Used with the <A> Tag

href=	Defines the target location of the hyperlink. This value can be any valid application type defined to the browser (such as http, ftp, mailto, and file).
name=	Defines a tag to be linked to through the use of a hyperlink tag. Allows positioning to a specific point within the page.
target=	Identifies where the link should be loaded when the link is displayed within a framed document (see the section on frames, below). A value of _blank forces the document to be loaded within a new browser window.

Document Formatting

<p></p>	Used to surround a defined paragraph.
 	Inserts a forced line break on the page.
<blockquote></blockquote>	Causes text contained within the group to be indented from both sides of the page.
<div></div>	Used to create groups of tags within a document.

Graphics	
<img>	Used to display an image file within the page.

Optional Attributes Used with the <IMG> Tag

src=	Defines the name of the graphic file to be loaded.
border=	Identifies the width of the border displayed around the image.
<hr>	Inserts a horizontal rule line on the page.

Optional Attributes Used with the <HR> Tag

size=	Sets the height of the rule line.
width=	Defines the width of the rule line.
noshade	Removes the shadow effect from the rule line.

Tables	
<table></table>	Used to define an HTML table.

Optional Attributes Used with the <TABLE> Tag

bgcolor=	Sets the background color of the table. Also available on <tr>, <td>, and <th>.
border=	Defines the width of the border line around each of the cells within the table.
cellpadding=	Sets the margin between the cell border and the contents.
cellspacing=	Sets the amount of space between the cells.
height=	Defines the height of a row, either in pixels or as a percent of the document height.
width=	Defines the table width, either in pixels or as a percent of the document width.
<tr></tr>	Defines the rows of a table. Must be between <table> and </table> tags.
<td></td>	Declares each cell within a table. Must be between <tr> and </tr> tags.
<th></th>	Defines header cells within a table. Must be between <tr> and </tr> tags.

Optional Attributes Used with the <TR>, <TD>, or <TH> Tags

align=	Defines horizontal alignment as left, right, or center.

207

valign=	Sets vertical alignment as top, middle, or bottom.
height=	Defines the height of a row, either in pixels or as a percent of the table height. (for <tr> only).

Optional Attributes Used with the <TD> or <TH> Tags Only

colspan=	Sets the number of columns a cell should span.
rowspan=	Sets the number of rows a cell should span.
nowrap=	Prevents column wrapping.
width=	Defines the cell width, either in pixels or as a percent of the table width.

HTML Frames

<frameset></frameset>   Defines a group of frames for a framed HTML page.

Optional Attributes Used with the <FRAMESET> Tag

rows=	Defines the number of rows in the frameset, either in pixels or as a percent of the width of the browser window.
cols=	Sets the number of columns in the frameset, either in pixels or as a percent of the width of the browser window.

<frame>   Defines individual frames within a frameset.

Optional Attributes Used with the <FRAME> Tag

src=	Points to the URL of the document to be displayed within the define frame.
name=	Names the frame for use with the *target* attribute on a hyperlink.
marginwidth=	Sets the left and right margins within the frame in pixels.
marginheight=	Defines the top and bottom margins for the frame in pixels.
scrolling=	Defines whether or not scroll bars are displayed for the frame, using values of Yes, No, or Auto. The Auto value automatically adds scroll-bars if required.
noresize	Prevents the frame from being resized within the browser.

Identifies what should be displayed in browsers that do not support frames.

HTML Forms

<form></form>	Used to declare an HTML form.

Optional Attributes Used with the \<FORM> Tag

name=	Identifies the name of the form.
action=	Defines the URL to which the form data should be passed.
method=	Defines how values should be passed to the URL defined on the *action* attribute. Valid values are POST, (to send data through the Form collection), or GET (to send values through the Querystring collection).

<input>	Defines an input element within an HTML form.

Optional Attributes Used with the \<INPUT> Tag

type=	Identifies the type of input element being defined. Valid values include, *text* for an input text field, *checkbox* for a check box, *radio* to create a radio button, *submit* to create the submit button, *reset* to create a reset button, and *img* to display a picture file that will act as a submit button.
name=	Defines the name of the input element.
size=	Sets the size of the input element.

<select></select>	Identifies a list box within an HTML form.

Optional Attributes Used with the \<SELECT> Tag

name=	Identifies the name of the list box field.
multiple	Indicates that multiple selections are allowed within this field.

<option value=> </option>	Defines each item within a list box, where *value* is the value to be passed.
<textarea ></textarea>	Creates a text area within the HTML form.

Optional Attributes Used with the \<TEXTAREA> Tag

name=	Identifies the field within the text area.
cols=	Sets the number of columns displayed within the text area.
rows=	Sets the number of rows displayed within the text area.

Appendix B

Sample Application
Installation Instructions

This information is intended to assist you in the installation of the examples included with this book. To download the files, go to our Website at *www.mcpressonline.com* and select **Site Help --> MC-Store.com Support --> MC Product Support --> Product Updates** and then select this book's title. With the exception of the complete applications in chapters 5 and 6, the ASP source should be placed in the root directory of the Web server. In the case of a Windows Web server running Microsoft Internet Information Server (IIS), this will usually be *d:*\Inetpub\wwwroot\, where *d:* represents the drive letter on which the root folder is located.

If you install the code on *d:*\Inetpub\wwwroot\, you can access any of the sample ASP or HTML documents using the following format:

```
http://webserver/page.asp
```

In this format, *webserver* represents the system name or IP address of your Web server, and *page.asp* represents the name of the HTML or ASP file.

For the order-entry application in chapter 5, you should extract the .zip file "AspOrders.zip" from the Web site, making sure to allow it to be extracted to the path defined in the archive. If you're using WinZip, this appears on the Extract dialog as "Use Folder Names."

The folder should be extracted to the drive containing your IIS root folder. This will automatically create the subfolders required for this example. Table B.1 describes the files used for this example.

Table B.1: Files Used by the Shopping Cart Application

File Name	Path Location	Description
adovbs.inc	*d:*\Inetpub\wwwroot\ASPOrders\	An Include file that defines ADO constant values.
catalog.asp	*d:*\Inetpub\wwwroot\ASPOrders\	An ASP to display item catalog.
createcust.asp	*d:*\Inetpub\wwwroot\ASPOrders\	An ASP that allows a user to enter customer information.
customermaint1.asp	*d:*\Inetpub\wwwroot\ASPOrders\	The first page of the customer-maintenance application.
customermaint2.asp	*d:*\Inetpub\wwwroot\ASPOrders\	Page two of the customer-maintenance application.
error.asp	*d:*\Inetpub\wwwroot\ASPOrders\	An ASP to display user error messages.
itemmaint1.asp	*d:*\Inetpub\wwwroot\ASPOrders\	The first page of the item master file maintenance.
itemmaint2.asp	*d:*\Inetpub\wwwroot\ASPOrders\	Page two of the item master file maintenance.
itemmaint3.asp	*d:*\Inetpub\wwwroot\ASPOrders\	Page three of the item master file maintenance.
include.asp	*d:*\Inetpub\wwwroot\ASPOrders\	An Include file that contains the HTML style sheet.
leftsel.gif	*d:*\Inetpub\wwwroot\ASPOrders\	Image files used to create the "tabbed" effect.

Table B.1: Files Used by the Shopping Cart Application, *continued*

leftunsel.gif	*d:*\Inetpub\wwwroot\ASPOrders\	
rightsel.gif	*d:*\Inetpub\wwwroot\ASPOrders\	
rightunsel.gif	*d:*\Inetpub\wwwroot\ASPOrders\	
NOImage.jpg	*d:*\Inetpub\wwwroot\ASPOrders\images	A JPEG image used by catalog.asp.
processord.asp	*d:*\Inetpub\wwwroot\ASPOrders\	An ASP that handles data access for order data.
shoppingcart.asp	*d:*\Inetpub\wwwroot\ASPOrders\	An ASP that allows a user to display and maintain the current contents of the shopping cart.
sidebar.inc	*d:*\Inetpub\wwwroot\ASPOrders\	An Include file that generates the side menu in the shopping-cart application.
validateuser.asp	*d:*\Inetpub\wwwroot\ASPOrders\	An ASP that handles user login and validation.

This example includes a modified version of the Adovbs.inc Include file. This file contains definitions for the following three constants, which are used within the application to connect to your data source:

- adUserid = "User" is the user ID used to access your data source.
- adPasswd= "secret" is the password associated with adUserid.
- adSystemIP= "192.168.0.1" is the IP address of your iSeries data source.

Each of these values should be modified to match valid values for your system. Each of the ASP source members for this application is slightly different than shown in the book. These pages have been modified to replace the hard-coded user ID, password, and system name values with the constant definitions mentioned here. To access the first page of this example, use the following URL, where *webserver* is the name or IP address of your Web server:

```
http://webserver/ASPOrders/catalog.asp
```

For the ad hoc sales-reporting application covered in chapter 6, you should extract the .zip file "SalesReporting.zip" from the Web site, again making sure to allow it to be extracted to the path defined in the archive. The folder should be extracted to the drive containing your IIS root folder. Table B.2 describes the files used in this example.

Table B.2: Files Used for the Ad Hoc Sales-Reporting Application

File Name	Path Location	Description
adovbs.inc	*d:*\Inetpub\wwroot\SalesReporting\	An Include file that defines ADO constant values.
blank.txt	*d:*\Inetpub\wwroot\SalesReporting\ SavedReportURLs\	A default file used for saving report definitions.
chart.jpg	*d:*\Inetpub\wwroot\SalesReporting\	An image file that displays a chart.
jscripts.js	*d:*\Inetpub\wwroot\SalesReporting\	The source file containing the client JavaScript code.
salesreport1.asp	*d:*\Inetpub\wwroot\SalesReporting\	An ASP that builds the report definition.
salesreport2.asp	*d:*\Inetpub\wwroot\SalesReporting\	An ASP that defines report sorting and grouping.
salesreport3.asp	*d:*\Inetpub\wwroot\SalesReporting\	An ASP that displays the finished report.
spreadsheet.asp	*d:*\Inetpub\wwroot\SalesReporting\	An ASP that displays report data in a spreadsheet format.
vbscripts.vbs	*d:*\Inetpub\wwroot\SalesReporting\	The source file containing the client-side VBScript code.

This example includes the same modified version of the Adovbs.inc Include file as the previous example. Again, the user ID, password, and system name values should be modified to match valid values for your system. The first page for this example would be accessed through the following URL, where webserver is the name or IP address of your Web server:

```
http://webserver/SalesReporting/salesreport1.asp
```

Index

Note: Boldface numbers indicate illustrations.